Eating for Life

Clemency Mitchell
Additional contributors: Lucinda Annan,
Agnes David, Angeline Francis, Huldah Ogwel,
and Thelma Soremekun

Copyright © The Stanborough Press Ltd 2017
Published by The Stanborough Press Ltd,
Grantham, England

All rights reserved. No part of this publication may be reproduced in any form without prior permission from the publisher.

British Library Cataloguing in Publication Data.
A catalogue record of this book is available from the British Library.

ISBN 978-1-78665-014-6

Certain recipes within this book have been republished, with permission, from the *Vegetarian Recipe Book*, copyright © Mary Namakando 2010, published by Hanwell Seventh-day Adventist Church (58-60 Greenford Avenue, Hanwell, London, England). The individual contributors of these recipes are listed on the title page of *Eating for Life*. The Stanborough Press Ltd gratefully acknowledges the help of Mary Namakando and Agnes David of Hanwell Seventh-day Adventist Church in bringing these recipes to a wider readership.

Pictures throughout this book are used for illustrative purposes only, and may not fully represent the completed recipes in every case.

Stock Photography:
©123RF.com
©iStockPhoto.com
©ingimage.com

Designed by David Bell.

Printed in Serbia.

Contents

Introduction  4

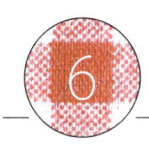 6 Getting started

Breakfasts  16

 50 Soups

Salads  82

 96 Main meals

Desserts  144

Introduction

Why another vegetarian cookbook? There are already plenty available, along with a growing number of vegan books. There are also a great many books about diet and health. This book combines tasty recipes with some very simple, scientifically proven health principles that may be used as part of a simple, whole plant-food diet. Together with adequate exercise and an optimistic frame of mind this will form the basis for a healthy lifestyle.

Who is this book for? It has been written for anyone who wants to improve their health and enjoy their food. It aims to help new vegetarians and vegans and anyone whose health would benefit by a change in eating.

What are my qualifications for writing a book like this? I worked as a general medical practitioner (GP) and taught college courses in health principles for many years. I've also taught nutrition and cookery courses to the general public and have cooked at home for a household varying from two to a dozen or more.

My years in general practice have taught me that a change in diet and lifestyle are the best prescription for most chronic health problems, and as a teacher I have had the opportunity to study nutrition and other health-related topics in more detail than many medical doctors are able to. Though this is not a therapeutic cookbook for specific problems, it's based on dietary principles that are of proven value in maintaining and restoring health.

My experience of cooking has made me appreciate recipes that are quick, easy and economical, as well as healthy and wholesome, and these factors have guided the choice of recipes in this book.

Nowadays we are bombarded with information about health, including numerous and varied nutritional theories that clamour for attention. The principles underlying this book are not based on these alone, but on timeless and trustworthy principles that are rooted in the Creator's plan for our diet. There we learn that the Creator designed a plant-food diet and an active lifestyle with a weekly rest day for the human race. Medical and nutritional science, common sense and experience, both in the kitchen and in the consulting room, confirm that these principles still hold the secrets of good health.

I have tried to share these timeless principles of healthy eating in an interesting and simple way that is easy to follow and put into practice. I hope you will enjoy reading the book as much as I did writing it.

Clemency Mitchell

Disclaimer
Although diet and nutrition are crucial to the maintenance and recovery of health, people can become ill even on the most perfect diet. The information in this book can have a very positive impact on your health, but it should not take the place of appropriate medical advice. It is usually best to make dietary changes gradually, and if you have medical problems and are on medication it is very important to discuss any major diet or lifestyle changes you plan to make with your doctor or other health advisor.

IMPORTANT: While all the dishes described in this book have been designed as healthy and delicious alternatives to meat and dairy foods, some ingredients, such as peanuts and cashews, may provoke an allergic reaction in sensitive individuals. Please enquire whether this is likely of any for whom you are catering, and make the necessary adjustments to their meal. Neither the author nor the publisher may be held responsible for any adverse consequences resulting from failure to follow this advice.

GETTING STARTED

Equipment

The simpler the food, the simpler the equipment needed. The absolute basics are a chopping board, a sharp knife, a grater, a good saucepan with a well-fitting lid and a sieve. Here are some other suggestions for what should be in the well-equipped vegetarian kitchen:

- **Measuring cups and spoons:** scales are seldom needed with this type of cooking.
- **A set of stainless steel saucepans,** including a **steamer** for cooking vegetables.
- **A blender with a coffee mill attachment.** This is a most important piece of electrical equipment for vegetarians and vegans. Cheap ones are as effective as expensive ones, but do not last as long. If you are planning to make your own nut butters regularly, it's worth

investing in an extra-strong one. A hand blender is useful, too. Food processors are also very useful, but not as vital as blenders.
- **A pressure cooker** is very useful for beans, chickpeas and other things that need long, slow cooking. **Slow cookers** can be used for the same things.
- **Ovenware:** ceramic or glass casserole dishes, pie dishes, baking trays and loaf tins.

The store cupboard
Here are a few suggestions about those things to have on hand.

Seasonings:
- Salt and herb salt such as Herbamare, vegetable stock cubes, yeast extract.
- Dried herbs such as mixed herbs, bouquet garni, dried basil, tarragon, oregano, freeze-dried parsley and dill.
- Mild spices such as coriander, cumin, cardamom and sweet Hungarian paprika. (In the interest of good digestion, black or red pepper, chillies and other irritant spices are only sparingly used in these recipes.)

Staple dry goods:
- **Cereals:** rice, whole cereal grains, flakes, including porridge oats, and flours – wholewheat for general use, unbleached white for occasional use, cornflour for thickening things.
- **Pulses:** lentils, beans and chickpeas if you have time to soak and cook them.
- **Nuts:** all kinds, but store large quantities in the freezer or fridge.
- **Seeds:** sunflower, sesame and pumpkin seeds and tahini. Store large amounts in fridge or freezer.
- **Dried fruit:** chopped dates, raisins, dried apricots.

Tins:
Tomatoes, tomato purée, beans, chickpeas and other pulses, and sweetcorn.

'Milks':
Soya milk and coconut milk (tins).

Olive oil:
Extra virgin cold-pressed for salads, standard olive oil for cooking. Store these out of direct sunlight.

Lemon juice.

The freezer
The vegetarian freezer is mainly used for storing items like berries, plums and apple sauce, vegetables like frozen peas and beans, nuts, seeds and other things that are much cheaper in bulk but don't keep forever on the shelf.

Shopping
There are plenty of healthy foods available in the major shops, but it is always a good idea to read the labels, especially when buying tinned or other processed products.

- **Fruits and vegetables:** the fresher, the more seasonal and the more locally produced, the better. Go to farm shops, local markets and 'pick your own' farms if you can. Organically grown is the very best, so long as it's fresh as well.
- **Packet cereals:** select those that are the most natural with no added sugar or salt. Be aware that almost all packaged cereals have added sugar and/or salt. Most of the crunchy oat cereals contain oil and lots of sugar.
- **Loose cereals for cooking:** porridge oats, brown rice, whole barley, cracked wheat.
- **Dried fruits:** raisins (preferably without added oil), apricots, dates, figs, pears, etc.
- **Nuts and seeds:** health food shops are also a good source of these products. Remember that roasted nuts usually have added oil and lots of salt.

- **'Milk'**: white, shop-brand, non-dairy milks are usually the cheapest and represent good value for money. The unsweetened type is the most versatile.
- **'Butter'**: peanut butter usually has added oil and sometimes sugar. Some supermarkets have tahini (sesame purée) at a reasonable price.
- **Jams**: you can often find a good selection of whole-fruit jams made with fruit juice rather than sugar.
- **Bread**: choose wholewheat, not just brown. Be sure that multigrain or granary loaves are made with whole, unrefined flour if you are going to eat them frequently.
- **Crispbreads**: there's usually a choice across the whole range of wholegrain crispbreads, but some are very salty.

Buying in bulk

Buying in bulk can save a lot of money if the foods have a long shelf life. Nuts, seeds, tahini and apple juice concentrate are often good-value bulk buys. Storage is important: a dark, cool, dry cupboard for cereal grains and other dry staples with low fat content. Nuts and seeds do not keep so well because of their high fat content, so store them in a fridge or freezer. Some dried fruits are liable to ferment if kept for a long time, as is apple juice concentrate once it's opened, so keep it in the fridge.

What about organic food?

There is a growing range of available organic foods these days but they are usually a lot more expensive. Research results are conflicting, some showing quite a difference in nutritional value, others none at all. This much is clear: plant foods, however they are grown, contain valuable health-promoting substances not found in foods of animal origin. They also contain much lower levels of pesticide residues than animal foods do. Organic agriculture is the most natural and the ideal would be for us to grow our own food in our own organic gardens, but few of us are able to do this now. Those who don't have the opportunity to have the best can take comfort in

the fact that a healthy lifestyle with a wide range of plant foods will do a great deal to compensate for the pollutants that we are unable to avoid.

Measurements

Standard cup and spoon measurements are used in this book. Occasionally other measurements are used for ingredients that come in packets or tins. Measuring cups are usually much quicker to use than scales, and are especially useful for plant-food cookery, which tends to be more flexible, and doesn't often need exact measurements.

1 cup = 250ml (one standard teacup)
½ cup = 125ml
¼ cup = 62.5ml (roughly 4 Tbs)
1 standard tablespoon (1 Tbs) = 15ml (old-fashioned tablespoon)
1 standard teaspoon (1 tsp) = 5ml (old-fashioned teaspoon)

Here are a few guide measurements:
1 cup flour weighs about 6oz or 170g
1 cup porridge oats weighs about 4oz or 112g
1 cup rice weighs just over 6oz or 170g
1 cup peanuts weighs about 6oz or 170g
1 cup cashews weighs about 5oz or 140g
1 cup brown sugar weighs about 6oz or 170g
1 cup honey weighs about 4oz or 126g
1 cup table margarine weighs about 4oz or 112g

Cooking times and ovens

Cooking times depend on the type of oven used, its temperature, the position of the food in it, the size and thickness of the food to be cooked and the container the food is in. Exact timing and temperature are not so important for most of the recipes in this book, and in view of all the different kinds of ovens and all the different kinds of ovenware, they have not been given.

If things are not cooking as fast as you want, turn up the heat, and, if necessary, cover the food with foil to prevent the top from browning too much. Fan ovens produce an even heat, and the food cooks appreciably faster. Non-fan ovens are hotter at the top, so it is important which shelf you use. When cooking things for the first time, plan for a little extra cooking time, and check the food from time to time. Below is a general guide to oven temperatures:

Heat level	Degrees Fahrenheit	Degrees Centigrade	British Gas Mark
Very cool	200-250	95-120	0-1
Cool	275-300	135-150	1-2
Warm	325	165	3
Moderate	350-375	175-190	4-5
Hot	400-425	200-220	6-7
Very hot	450-475	230-245	8-9

Explanatory notes about ingredients

These recipes only use plant foods. A few concentrated things are used, like yeast extract for flavouring, apple juice concentrate for sweetening and cornflour for thickening, but most of the ingredients are simple, natural and unrefined. Most of the recipes are flexible in both ingredients and quantities, so you can adapt them according to your taste and need.

Salt

Human beings need some salt. The fact that the unhealthy Western diet contains too much salt is not a reason to banish it altogether. Our appetites demand the amount of salt we are used to, and it isn't difficult to retrain them. You can painlessly reduce your salt intake over the course of a few weeks, giving your taste buds time to adjust. Salt is not necessary in many neutral and sweet foods, such as cooked breakfast cereals, granola, cookies and other baked goods, so it is not included in any of the recipes for these things.

In most of the savoury recipes you will find the instruction 'salt to taste' because the amount of salt you want to add is clearly a matter of taste.

Which type of salt? Choose natural sea salt for its extra trace minerals.

Seasoning

Flavourings are also a matter of personal taste, which is why many of these recipes say 'season to taste'. We recommend herbs and milder spices rather than the strong, hot, spicy seasonings. Herb salt, vegetable stock cubes, bouillon powder and such things are all useful seasonings, usually containing as much salt as your dish will need.

Yeast extract

This is a very good salty flavouring for soups and stews.

Soy sauce

Check labels carefully if you are concerned about this, or if you use it

often. The unfermented MSG-free variety is the healthiest.

Yeast flakes
These are usually available in health food shops. They add flavour, are rich in B-complex vitamins and are a useful addition to many vegetarian recipes.

Onions and garlic
These feature in a lot of recipes. They are full of important health-promoting phytochemicals, but you can omit them if you want to. If there isn't time to peel, chop or press, replace fresh onions with onion flakes or powder, and fresh garlic with garlic granules, powder or purée.

Sweetening
Dates and raisins are ideal whole-food sweeteners. Apple juice concentrate, honey, maple syrup and raw cane sugar are unrefined, but are very concentrated, and in limited amounts there is little to choose between them. None of them is recommended in large amounts. For those with weight or other health problems it will be best to use dried fruits as sweeteners. Strict vegans will query the use of honey, but it is included because it is a plant-based food naturally processed by bees.

Fats and oils
Human beings need natural fats and oils. The key word is *natural*, as they should be those found in nuts, seeds, olives and avocados. Once they are refined and processed they tend to be overused, and there may be special problems caused by the refining process. At high temperatures the structure of some of the fat molecules alters to the infamous trans-fats associated

with various kinds of tissue damage and health problems. This can occur during home cooking, too: for example, in deep-fat frying and baking.

The ideal way to eat fats and oils is in their natural state, as they come in whole plant foods. Those who need to lose weight or have other serious health problems are recommended to try a diet free of all added fats, with the possible exception of a strictly limited amount of olive oil.

Olive oil does not have the problems of other vegetable oils, as it is stable at high temperatures, and has health-promoting properties as well. The most natural is the extra virgin cold-pressed olive oil, but cheaper olive oils are good too. Choose the best olive oil for salads and recipes where flavour is important, and the cheaper ones for other things. Olive oil is considerably more expensive than refined vegetable oils, but the sort of healthy diet recommended in this book uses very much less oil than the ordinary diet, so its use is not extravagant.

Plant food alternatives

'**Milk**' – Unsweetened soya milk, nut milk, or any other plant food milk.

'**Cheese**' – This means any 100% vegetarian recipe that can be used as dairy cheese would be.

'**Cream**' – Any 100% vegetarian recipe with a creamy consistency that can be used instead of dairy cream.

Agar takes the place of gelatine – get it at your health food shop.

TVP (textured vegetable protein, made from soya) – mince and chunks and other sorts of vegetarian meat don't feature very much in this book, but they occasionally have their place, especially during the transition to a vegetarian diet.

BREAKFASTS

Introduction

Breakfast is **very important**. According to Mrs Beeton, the great English cookery writer, the moral and physical well-being of mankind depends largely upon its breakfast; and we have all heard the saying, sometimes attributed to Hippocrates, that we should 'breakfast like a king, lunch like a prince, and sup like a pauper'.

Eating breakfast is one of the seven health habits most closely associated with longevity, as important as regular exercise and not smoking. Workers who eat breakfast are more efficient; schoolchildren who eat breakfast are calmer and get better grades.

Thousands of researchers have confirmed these and many other benefits of a nourishing breakfast, including better concentration at school and work, even-temperedness, better behaviour, better control of blood sugar, weight and cholesterol, a stronger immune system and more chance of avoiding addictions.

For optimum performance, our bodies, like cars at the start of a trip, need a good supply of appropriate fuel to begin the day. For us, getting the best from our food, it needs to look good and taste good, we need the right amount at the right time, and it does us more good if we eat it in a cheerful frame of mind.

This book provides a variety of suggestions to keep breakfast interesting, whether you want your breakfast to be quick and cheerful for weekdays or leisurely and luxurious for weekends or holidays.

'Grains, fruits, nuts, and vegetables constitute the diet chosen for us by our Creator. These foods, prepared in as simple and natural a manner as possible, are the most healthful and nourishing. They impart a strength, a power of endurance, and a vigour of intellect, that are not afforded by a more complex and stimulating diet.' Ellen G. White, *Counsels on Diet and Foods*, p. 363.

This is a **vegetarian** cookbook. More than that, it is a **strict vegetarian** cookbook. Only plant foods are used, and usually whole plant foods at that. That simply means grains, fruits, nuts, seeds and vegetables prepared in simple, natural ways. The healing properties of plant foods are the reason for the generally longer and healthier lives of vegetarians and vegans.

Although breakfast traditions vary vastly from country to country, the underlying principles of good nutrition are the same. Unrefined starches – breads and cereals, made from whole grains – are basic, along with small amounts of more concentrated foods like seeds and nuts and, VERY IMPORTANT, plenty of fruits and vegetables.

The important thing is that most of the food should be simple, natural and unrefined.

The recipes here are for a variety of whole, unrefined, plant-based breakfast dishes that are easy to make and flexible enough to be adapted and used wherever whole, unrefined plant foods are available.

Solutions to some common breakfast problems
'Can't face breakfast': cut down on your evening meal and start with a very small breakfast, such as a banana or apple, and gradually build up.
'No time to cook in the morning': don't cook; eat fruit, bread and spreads. Use packaged ready-to-eat cereals or cook the night before and reheat.
'Don't like cereals': then eat fruit and a variety of breads and spreads.
'Absolutely no time to eat breakfast': in the long term, change your programme and get up earlier. In the short term, grab some fruit to eat on the way (or you could make a sandwich the night before).
'Can't be bothered fiddling about with recipes': eat bread with a handful of nuts and raisins and go for convenience fruits like apples and bananas.

A guide to choosing breakfast menus
A continental breakfast is a quick, light breakfast, which can be anything from tea and toast to bread with an array of spreads, cereals, orange juice, yoghurt and fresh fruit. It varies from country to country.

In France it may be just bread and coffee (croissants on Sundays), but in Germany they add cheese and sliced sausage, and in Hungary there can be tomatoes, cucumber and radishes as well.

A cooked breakfast usually means something savoury to eat with a knife and fork. There are healthy and tasty alternatives to the traditional fry-up with its high content of animal fat and protein.

Another option is the **'everyday healthy plant-food breakfast'**: whole cereal with bread, spreads and fruit.

- **Choose fresh fruit** – have some every day if you can and at least four different kinds each week, choosing seasonal varieties when possible.
- **Cereals** – ring the changes by alternating between packet cereals and home-cooked varieties. The different cereal grains each contain their own collection of nutrients and phytochemicals, so vary them from day to day.
- **Cereal toppings** – make cereals much more interesting by having a selection of half a dozen things to add to them – granola, pumpkin seeds, coconut, chopped dates, raisins, chopped or ground nuts, ground flaxseed.
- **Instead of cow or goat milk** – use soya, nut, coconut or oat milk, stewed fruit or fruit sauce with dry or cooked cereals.
- **Breads** – vary your wholewheat with nonwheat crispbread, rye bread or oatcakes.
- **Spreads** – try making your own, or buy a couple of whole-nut or seed butters so that you can use two or three varieties in the week. Tapenade is a delicious savoury spread made from olives that the ancient Romans used instead of butter.
- **Fruit spreads** – buy or make your own. Mashed banana makes a very good butter and jam substitute, and avocado is known as 'nature's butter'.

Three 'everyday healthy plant-based breakfast' menus to help you get started on the better breakfast plan . . .

1. **Fresh fruit** – apples and bananas
   Cereal – shredded wheat in whatever packaged form you have available
   Topping – granola, raisins, and half a sliced banana
   'Milk' – soya or other non-dairy milk
   Bread – wholewheat toast
   Spread – nut butter and the rest of the banana, mashed

2. **Fresh fruit** – 2-3 apricots, 2-3 strawberries
   Cereals – cooked brown rice flakes
   Topping – chopped dates and shredded coconut, apple purée
   Oatcakes
   Spreads – peanut butter, Marmite or similar yeast spread

3. **Fresh fruit and cereal** – Cool and creamy oatmeal (see p. 29)
   Bread – wholewheat toast
   Spreads – tahini and apricot 'jam', tapenade (olive paste spread)

An important nutritional supplement: ground flaxseed

Few people need to buy vitamin or mineral supplements. But it makes sense to supplement your diet with some extra-specially nutritious whole-plant-food items.

Chia and flaxseed are rich plant sources of the omega-3 fats that are important for the brain and immune system, so they are valuable additions to breakfast. Grind some fresh each day in a coffee mill and sprinkle over breakfast cereals. For extra flavour, grind some coriander or caraway seeds with it.

Cooked cereals

Breakfast is a good time for eating cereals – not just packet cereals or porridge, but everything made from cereal grains.

Whole cereals contain many important vitamins, minerals, phytochemicals and fibre, many of which are lost when they are refined. For strong nerves, healthy bones, a strong immune system and good digestion, choose whole varieties, whether in packaged or hot cooked cereals or in bread.

Cook cereals well. Whole grains of wheat need several hours; whole barley, at least an hour; brown rice, 50 minutes; millet, 45-50 minutes. Rolled or flaked cereals cook much faster, particularly rolled oats, which are already partly cooked. Meal, for example cornmeal, cooks even quicker.

Do not eat cereals raw, with the possible exception of oats that have been soaked overnight. Well-cooked grains are more nourishing as well as more digestible, so, if anything, err on the side of overcooking them.

Quantities: as a rough guide, reckon on half a cup of uncooked cereal or a cup of cooked cereal per person.

Oat porridge for two people
1 cup porridge oats to 2½ cups water

- Bring to the boil, stirring occasionally, then turn down heat and simmer for 5 minutes.
- Add more water if you like a thinner porridge.

Some like their porridge plain with non-dairy milk and a little salt, and I have even heard of porridge being eaten with a commercial or homemade savoury relish. Some suggestions for a delicious bowl of porridge: top with sliced banana, raisins, chopped nuts or granola, ground flaxseed and soya milk and/or soya cream.

Sweet tooth? Drizzle a little honey, maple syrup, apple juice concentrate or black treacle over the top.

Cooking other cereal flakes
Rice and millet flakes: 1 cup flakes to 2-3 cups water (depending on how thick you want it to be). Make in the same way as oat porridge but cook for about 10 minutes.
Wheat, barley and rye flakes: same proportions, but cook for longer. Barley flakes need at least 20 minutes.
Cracked wheat: cook for 5-10 minutes or simply pour boiling water over it and let it stand for 15 minutes.
Time-saving tip: pour boiling water over cereal flakes and leave for half an hour or longer. This will greatly reduce the time needed to cook them.

Hot cooked cereal variations
- **Piña colada rice** – for 1 cup brown rice flakes add 1 cup tinned crushed pineapple and ½ cup shredded coconut and reduce the water by ½ cup.
- **Armenian barley** – to 1 cup barley flakes add ½ cup chopped dried apricots, ½ cup raisins and ½ teaspoon (tsp) ground coriander.
- **Danish rye** – to 1 cup rye flakes add ½ tsp caraway seeds and 1 tablespoon (Tbs) black molasses.

BREAKFAST RECIPES
SPECIAL CEREAL DISHES

Here are some delicious breakfast dishes for when you need a change, or when you have more time. You can make most of them partly or completely in advance, and re-heat them in the morning.

Breakfast bread or rice pudding

½ cup cashews
½ cup dates
1½ cups hot water
½ tsp cinnamon
½ tsp vanilla
½ cup chopped walnuts
½ cup raisins
2 cups cooked brown rice, or 3 cups wholewheat bread cut in ½-inch (1.5cm) cubes

- Blend the cashews, dates and water thoroughly, add the cinnamon and vanilla, then pour over the rice or bread cubes mixed with chopped nuts and raisins and bake in a medium-deep dish in an oven on moderate heat for 30-40 minutes.
- Serve with sliced banana and non-dairy milk or cream. Serves 4.

Millet crumble

1½ cups cooked millet
1½ cups orange or pineapple juice
Granola
Bananas

- Blend the first two ingredients until creamy. (This works best if the mixture is hot – use freshly cooked millet, or heat the fruit juice.)
- Take a baking dish, 8 inches (20cm) square or similar size, and put a layer of granola on the bottom.
- Cover this with a layer of sliced bananas. Pour the hot millet mixture over the bananas and top with a thin layer of granola.
- Serve at once or heat in a moderate oven for 10-15 minutes. Serves 4.

Fruit crisp topping

¼ cup honey or apple juice concentrate
¼ cup oil
¼ cup water
1 tsp ground coriander
½ tsp vanilla essence
2¾ cups rolled oats
¼ cup wholewheat flour
½ cup coconut or chopped nuts

Filling

- Use sliced apples or a mixture of fruits, fresh and dried, to fill a large baking dish (8 inches/20cm square) three-quarters full.
- If the fruit is tart, sweeten with chopped dates, apple juice concentrate, pineapple juice or honey.
- With fresh fruit the liquid should come a quarter-way up the dish, halfway up if dried fruit is added.
- Mix the topping ingredients together and sprinkle over the filling.
- Bake in a moderately hot oven for 45 minutes or until the top is golden brown.
- Serve with nut cream or 'milk'. Serves 6.

Baked oatmeal

1¼ cups porridge oats
½ cup raisins
½ cup chopped nuts
1½ cups apple juice
½ tsp cinnamon
¼ tsp vanilla essence
2 large apples, chopped

- Mix thoroughly, and bake in a medium-deep casserole dish for 1 hour in a moderately hot oven.
- Serve with nut or soya milk or cream. Serves 4.

Muesli

Contrary to what most people think, muesli as it's usually eaten here is not a healthy dish. The original muesli, invented by Dr Bircher Benner more than a hundred years ago, was thoroughly soaked overnight to ensure that the grains were digestible, and the bulk of the dish was the fresh raw fruit that was added in the morning. Dr Bircher Benner would hardly recognise the indigestible raw flakes and scant dried fruit and nuts called muesli now.

Here is a variation on muesli:
Cool and creamy oatmeal
2 cups porridge oats
2 cups orange juice
½ cup chopped nuts
4-6 cups fresh fruit

- Combine the first three ingredients and refrigerate overnight.
- Just before serving, mix in the prepared fresh fruit, such as grated apples, chopped pears, peaches or apricots and berries. Serves 4.

Cooked muesli
Cooked muesli makes a delicious hot cereal. Choose one of the dairy-free muesli mixes with added fruit and nuts.
- Those coarse cereal grains need quite a lot of cooking. The quickest method is to pour boiling water over it and let it soak for ½-1 hour, then cook for 15-30 minutes.
- Use a generous half-cup of dry muesli per person and 2-3 times the volume of water, depending on how thick or thin you want it to be.
- Serve with nut or soya milk or cream.

Granola

Granola is delicious, easy to make and keeps well in an airtight box or tin.

- These recipes are very flexible. You can vary the cereal part, using whatever whole cereal flakes you can find (such as millet, rye, wheat) with whatever nuts and seeds you have.
- You can use oil, nut or seed butter, or nuts or seeds ground up with water.
- Sweetening can be honey, malt, fruit juice concentrate or mashed bananas, apple sauce or soft brown sugar.
- The nuts are best slightly chopped, and seeds like sesame or flax are better ground.
- The proportions can be varied, but just be sure to have a crumbly texture, avoiding big lumps because they take longer to cook.
- If you want to include raisins or any other dried fruit, add them after cooking or they will become hard.
- Add a tiny bit of salt if you want to, but it isn't really necessary for most tastes.
- Cook slowly, say at 120°C, checking and stirring occasionally.
- Granola made with oil will brown much more quickly, so needs more careful watching.

Oil-free granola 1

4 cups porridge oats
½ cup coconut
½ cup pumpkin or sunflower seeds
¾ cup chopped nuts, blended with just enough water to cover them
1 tsp vanilla
3-4 Tbs apple juice concentrate

- Mix together thoroughly and spread on two baking trays.
- Bake in a slow oven until golden-brown and crunchy.
- Check and stir occasionally while baking.

Oil-free granola 2

1-1¼ cups pitted dates, softened in enough hot water to cover them
2 ripe bananas
8 cups rolled oats
1 cup chopped nuts
1 cup coconut
1 cup sunflower seeds
½ tsp vanilla essence

- Blend the first two ingredients until smooth, then mix thoroughly with everything else.
- Spread about ½-inch thick on trays and bake in a cool oven for about 1½ hours, stirring occasionally.

Crunchy granola

2 cups porridge oats
2 cups jumbo oats
½ cup chopped walnuts
½ cup coconut
½ cup pumpkin seeds
¼ cup apple juice concentrate or honey
¼ cup oil
½ tsp vanilla

- Whisk the last three ingredients together and add to the rest.
- Mix well.
- Spread evenly on a baking tray and bake in a slow oven, checking every 15 minutes until it is golden-brown and crunchy.

Quick and easy waffles for a weekend breakfast treat

Waffles are quick and easy if you have the right equipment, and can easily be made for breakfast. They can also be made in advance and are very easily reheated in the waffle iron, in a toaster or in the oven or microwave.

This recipe is 100% natural whole food.

Waffles
1 cup sunflower seeds blended smooth in 1 cup water
1 cup porridge oats
1 cup wholewheat flour
3 cups water

- Blend everything together and cook in a waffle iron until golden brown.
- The batter thickens as it stands, so add more water if it gets too thick to pour easily.
- This recipe makes about 6 8cm-x-8cm waffles.

Very light oat waffles
2 cups water or non-dairy milk
2 cups porridge oats
2 Tbs sesame seeds
2 Tbs flour (wholewheat or any kind)
1-2 Tbs oil
1-2 Tbs honey (optional)

- Make in the same way as previous recipe.
- Yield: around 6 waffles.

Eat waffles with any of the delicious spreads that you enjoy eating on toast or bread, including fruit spreads, apple sauce, thick coconut cream, tahini with honey, maple syrup, etc. Or have savoury waffles with hummus, scrambled tofu, fried tomatoes or anything else that tastes good on bread or toast.

'MILKS' AND OTHER THINGS TO EAT WITH CEREALS

Soya milk is very widely available now, and generally inexpensive. If you have a large household who all use soya milk, however, a soya milk machine is a good investment, as milk can be made for a tenth of what it costs to buy. (These machines are very useful for making tofu, too.)

It is best not to use the same sort of milk every day, especially if you are avoiding dairy milk because of allergies. You could develop an allergy to soya milk, so vary the menu, and have a different milk or a fruit sauce from time to time.

Coconut is another delicious non-dairy 'milk'.

Cashew 'milk' or cream
- Blend 1 cup cashews in 1 cup water until very smooth – for about 1 minute, less if you cook them for a few minutes first.
- Add 3-4 cups water and blend again, briefly, for milk. Add proportionately less for cream.
- You can use other nuts, such as Brazil nuts or almonds, but cashews are the creamiest.

Cashew rice or oat 'milk'
½ cup cashews
½ cup cooked brown rice or cooked oats (leftover porridge)

- Add enough water to cover and blend until smooth, then add water as in previous recipe.
- Stir before serving.

Sesame 'milk'
- Blend light tahini together with 4 or 5 times that amount of water.
- Add more water as desired.

This is rather an acquired taste, but those who do acquire the taste love it. It's a rich source of calcium.

Sweetening 'milk'
Those who want to can sweeten their milk with a little apple juice concentrate, honey or malt, or blend in a couple of softened dates. A little vanilla or almond essence can be added too.

Fruit whip
- Blend together 1 cup pineapple or orange juice with a banana and use as milk with breakfast cereal.

Apple sauce
- The quickest way is to wash and roughly chop any sort of apples.
- Cook them with a little water until soft. Transfer to blender and whizz briefly.
- Sieve for a smooth and wholesome apple sauce.
- No blender? Cut the pieces a little smaller and cook for a little longer before sieving.

37

38

Breads

It's good to ring the changes with breads, especially now that wheat sensitivities are becoming so common. Try eating breads with more than one type of grain. As a refined food that has lost many of its nutrients as well as its healthy fibre, white bread should be substituted with less-refined varieties.

As with all the other breakfast foods, variety is good. Don't only eat wholewheat bread, but vary it sometimes with rye bread, mixed-grain bread, crispbreads, oatcakes or rice cakes.

Sufferers of coeliac disease have a sensitivity to gluten, which is a protein found in barley, wheat, rye, and other cereals such as durum wheat, bulgur wheat, emmer, and even spelt, as well as couscous and semolina. Breads made with these should therefore be avoided by coeliac sufferers, unless the gluten has been removed. Happily, corn and polenta are naturally gluten-free. Oats can also be tolerated, if not contaminated. See the Coeliac UK website (*www.coeliac.org.uk*) for more details.

'BUTTERS'

Butter is high in saturated fat and cholesterol, and margarine is a refined and processed product that often contains milk solids and sometimes unhealthy fats.

Even when you read the labels carefully and avoid hydrogenated oils, trans fats and milk solids, you still have an unnatural product, not ideal for an unrefined plant-food diet.

So what can take their place? Nuts and seeds are naturally high in very healthy oils and make very good whole-food butters.

Peanut butter is available everywhere, but read the labels and choose the whole-nut ones without added sugar, oil and salt.

Health food shops usually have a variety of nut butters but they tend to be expensive.

Tahini is sesame purée and it is quite widely available.

Nut butters
- Make small quantities in a coffee grinder or blender.
- Use either raw or roasted nuts. Cashews, peanuts, almonds and hazelnuts make particularly good butters if they are roasted first. (Put them on a tray in a hot oven or under the grill, and watch them carefully as they burn easily.)
- Walnuts, pecans and Brazil nuts make good butters just as they are.
- To make a small amount of nut butter, grind ¼ cup nuts to a fine powder in a coffee grinder.
- You may need to add some water or oil to make it spreadable.
- Add just enough to give it the right consistency.
- Adding water gives an excellent creamy spread that keeps for a few days in the fridge.
- If you use oil rather than water, it will keep for much longer.
- To make nut butter in a blender, grind up one cupful of nuts at a time and add water or oil as needed.

Seed butters
Tahini is sesame seed purée. It keeps very well and as it is very concentrated it goes a long way.

Some people love this thick grey paste straight away. Others need time to acquire the taste, but it's well worth doing so, as tahini is rich in calcium and healthy fats.

Some find it easier to spread if it is creamed by slowly stirring in an equal volume of water. (Just cream a small amount at a time, as it doesn't keep for long once water is added.)

You could easily make your own tahini with toasted sesame seeds in the coffee grinder in the same way as nut butters. You can make sunflower and pumpkin seed butters in the same way.

Two of the healthiest and most delicious butters:

Avocado butter
Ripe avocado is a delicious replacement for butter or cream cheese. Simply spread it generously onto your bread.

It goes well with savoury spreads like yeast extract, and is very good topped with sliced tomato or onion.

To make a spread for several people to share, mash a ripe avocado with a little chopped onion, some crushed garlic or garlic purée and salt to taste.

Avocado is also very good with sweet spreads, especially dark fruit spreads.

Banana butter

Just spread fresh ripe banana generously on your bread.

This is very good with nut butter or tahini, and with all kinds of fruit spreads and fresh fruit like berries, grapes or pear, peach or apricot slices.

Avocado banana butter

- Mash equal quantities of each together.
- Spread thickly on bread and eat right away. It doesn't keep.

FRUIT SPREADS

There are all kinds of interesting whole-food alternatives to butter, margarine and jam.

Dried fruit jams
- You can use one or more kinds of dried fruit. For soft, 'ready-to-eat' dried fruit, you can just pour boiling water over it and let it soak until it's soft, then mash or blend.
- For more chewy dried fruit, you may like to cook it as well.
- Soak first, for an hour or more, then cook gently until it's fairly soft, then mash or blend, or eat it on bread, just as it is.

Date spread
1 cup chopped dates with enough hot water to cover

- Just soak until soft and stir.

Variations: use orange juice instead of water; stir in ¼ tsp ground aniseed.

Orange fig spread
- Cook dried figs with enough orange juice to cover them, then blend (add more juice if necessary, but just enough to let the blender blades turn).

Apricot pear spread
- Cook a mixture of dried apricots and dried pears in enough water to cover them.
- Mash or blend, depending on how smooth you like it to be.

Raw fruit on bread
Bananas are perfect for spreading just as they come; so is ripe sharon fruit (persimmon), which has the consistency of jam.
   Other fresh fruits like peaches, pears and apricots can be cut up and arranged on mashed banana or on nut-buttered bread.

Here's a summer breakfast fit for a king – or a foodie
- Spread bread with nut butter, then with pear and raspberry purée fruit spread; cover with mashed banana and top with fresh raspberries or halved grapes. It's delicious!

Fresh or frozen fruit jams
- Use any sort of fresh or frozen fruit you like.
- Cook briefly and use chopped dates or raisins to sweeten and thicken: 1 cup dates to 1-2 cups fruit, depending on how sweet the fruit is.

Blackcurrant spread
1 cup fresh blackcurrants (use slightly more if using frozen fruit)
1 cup chopped dates
Water – just enough to cover the dates

- Cook the dates in the water for a few minutes, then add the fresh or frozen fruit, bring it to the boil, stir well, then leave it to cool.
- It will thicken as it cools.
- Add more water for a thinner spread.

Blackberry and cranberry spread
- As above, but use a mixture of cranberries and blackberries instead of blackcurrants.

Cranberry special
1 cup frozen cranberries (use slightly less for fresh cranberries)
¼ cup apple juice concentrate or honey
¼ cup raisins
¼ cup water

- Cook together until the cranberries have popped.

SAVOURY HOT BREAKFASTS

How about a totally vegetarian hot savoury breakfast at the weekend? These recipes are good to eat on toast. You can add mushrooms (sauté lightly in a little olive oil, and sprinkle with dried tarragon), vegetarian sausages, and perhaps some potatoes.

How about greens at breakfast? Bubble and squeak is easy, too.

Scrambled tofu
1 large onion, chopped
1 stick celery, chopped
2 Tbs olive oil with 1 Tbs water
1 250g block tofu
1 clove garlic, crushed
1 Tbs yeast flakes
1 tsp herb salt
¼ tsp turmeric

- Sauté the first three ingredients together until soft and transparent, then mash or blend before adding the crumbled tofu and seasonings.
- Mix well and heat through.

Easy beans
- Sauté a chopped onion, chopped celery stick and crushed garlic clove in olive oil until soft.

- Add several cups tinned or pre-cooked beans, 1 tin chopped tomatoes, 2 Tbs tomato purée, seasonings such as paprika, cumin, fresh coriander.
- Cook gently through and serve with fresh or grilled tomatoes or mushrooms.

Tomatoes Provençal
- Gently sauté a medium-sized onion, chopped or sliced, with a crushed clove of garlic.
- Add several thickly sliced fresh tomatoes or a tin of whole tomatoes, sprinkle with fresh or dried basil, cook gently through, season to taste and serve on toast or with scrambled tofu.

Bubble and squeak
This traditional British dish is simply leftover mashed potatoes and cooked cabbage fried together. Exact proportions are not important. The healthiest way to do this is to use minimal olive oil in a non-stick frying pan, or to simply mix it all up, put it in a shallow oven-proof dish and brown it in the oven. Chopped onion and crushed garlic add phytochemicals and give an extra tang.

'Vegan cheese'
Dairy cheese is a versatile and convenient food that has long been a part of the traditional Western diet.

Now we are learning more and more of the dangers of dairy produce, cheese begins to look less attractive. All dairy produce is naturally rich in reproductive and growth hormones, and the more mature the cheese, the more oxidised and dangerous the cholesterol.

Leaving out cheese can leave a big gap in a vegetarian cook's repertoire, so here are some completely plant-based alternatives. They can be used as spreads and sauces, toppings, and can even be made into sliceable blocks.

These 'vege-cheeses' have several advantages. Firstly, they lack the high saturated fat and cholesterol levels of dairy produce, with their worrying connections with specific serious diseases. Secondly, they also lack the irritant substances that cause food sensitivities such as migraines, indigestion and irritable bowel syndrome in susceptible people. Thirdly, and most importantly, they contain the health-promoting phytochemicals that occur naturally in their plant-derived ingredients.

Country Life cashew pimento 'cheese'
Blend until smooth:
1 cup water
¾ cup cashew nuts or sunflower seeds
2 Tbs sesame seeds or tahini
⅔ cup rolled oats
3 Tbs yeast flakes
1 small onion
1 level tsp herb salt
1 clove garlic
2 Tbs lemon juice, or to taste
½ cup tinned or fresh pimentos (sweet peppers)
⅛ tsp dill seed (optional)

This can be used as it is in lasagne, for pizza topping, or 'cheese' on toast. To make a spread, cook it until it thickens, stirring all the time.
- For 'cheese' on toast, spread generously and grill.
- To make into a brick for slicing, mix 4 Tbs agar flakes in 1½ cups water and boil until flakes are dissolved.
- Use the above recipe, but substitute the 1½ cups agar mixture for the 1 cup water.
- Blend until creamy, then pour into a mould and chill.

Quick 'cheese' sauce

1 cup cashew pieces cooked for a few minutes in 1 cup water
3 Tbs yeast flakes
1 tsp salt
¼ cup fresh onion
1 clove garlic
½ cup pimento (leave out if you would like a white 'cheese')
2 Tbs lemon juice

- Blend until very creamy.
- For 'cheese' on toast, spread it thickly on toast and grill until lightly browned.
- See below for pita pizza.
- For a 'cheese' spread that will keep for several days, cook, stirring constantly, until it thickens.

Pita pizza

This is a very quick and easy kind of pizza, which can quite easily be made for breakfast.

- Carefully split each piece of wholewheat pita bread into its two layers and spread each layer with pizza toppings.
- Start with a thin layer of tomato sauce if you have it: if not, use tomato or sun-dried tomato paste.
- The 'cheese' can come next, and on top of this can go all sorts of sliced things – onions, peppers, tomatoes, mushrooms, artichoke hearts, vegetarian sausage; or the 'cheese' can come last, spread or drizzled in a pattern over the top.
- A few olives and a sprinkle of oregano or other herbs complete it.
- Cook in a hot oven for 10-15 minutes and serve at once.

SAVOURY BREAKFAST SPREADS

Peanut butter or tahini with Marmite must be the easiest savoury breakfast spread. There are various vegetarian slicing sausages, pâtés and spreads to buy. Here are a few more to make at home. Serve them with bread, crispbread or toast, along with sliced tomatoes, cucumber, radishes or whatever else you fancy.

Bean spreads
You can give the blender a rest and simply mash the beans. There are endless variations to be made, so just use your imagination and whatever you can find in your cupboard. Here are two to start you off. Cook your own beans or open a tin.

Mediterranean: add olive oil, tomato purée, herbs – basil and/or oregano, chopped olives.

English special: mash the beans with a generous amount of Marmite. Mix well, and eat on toast.

Hummus
1 tin chickpeas (1½ cups)
1 cup tahini
1 small onion
1 clove garlic
3-5 Tbs lemon juice

- Blend, adding just enough water to allow blades to turn.
- Add salt to taste, and 2-3 Tbs olive oil if desired.
- Optional extras – add some chopped fresh red pepper, sweet paprika powder or fresh herbs to the mixture in the blender.

Tapenade
Black or green pitted olives and olive oil are the basic ingredients. Optional extras to add to 1 tin (1½ cups) black or green pitted olives (drained):

1-2 garlic cloves (or equivalent garlic purée)
2 Tbs chopped onion
2-3 sun-dried tomatoes or 1 Tbs tomato purée

- Make it in a food processor or blender, or chop it finely by hand.
- It can be oil-free if you have a food processor, but a little oil makes it easier to hold together.
- If you use a blender, add just enough oil to allow the blades to turn easily.

49

SOUPS

Introduction

Soup can be anything from a light, clear starter for a four-course dinner, to something so thick and filling that it's a meal in itself. Soup is convenient to make as everything goes in the pot together, and it's healthy as this way of cooking conserves the vitamins and minerals.

Soup-based meals can be both filling and nourishing. Balance the liquid soup with something chewy – bread, crispbread, crackers or croutons. Add a salad or some fruit and you have turned your soup into a good main meal.

Here are a few easy and flexible recipes for different kinds of soups. You can vary the vegetables, the starchy ingredients, the seasonings or the thickness. Many of these recipes start with onion, celery and garlic, but any or all of these can be omitted if necessary. You can sauté these ingredients in a little oil and water first. Use olive oil, as it has a special, rich flavour, as well as health-promoting phytochemicals. For an oil-free version, just omit sautéing and cook everything together.

SOUP RECIPES
HEARTY SOUP BOWLS

These soups are quick to make, healthy and nutritious – and, almost as important, they're delicious!

A quick clear soup

1 medium-sized onion, finely chopped
1 stick celery, finely chopped
1 clove garlic, crushed, or ¼ tsp garlic powder
1 Tbs olive oil
1½ pints (scant 900ml) water
1 bouquet garni sachet or fresh or dried herbs to taste
½ cup finely sliced carrot
½ cup frozen peas
½ cup sliced water chestnuts
Vegetable stock cube or herb salt to taste

- Sauté the onion, celery and garlic in the olive oil, with 1 Tbs water.
- When it's soft, add the boiling water, plus the carrots and seasoning.
- When the carrots are almost cooked, add the frozen peas and the water chestnuts.
- Simmer for a few minutes longer.

Variations on clear soup: add different vegetables, like thin slices of sweet peppers, courgettes, sliced mushrooms, or thin slices of vegetarian sausage.

Variations on flavouring and colour – add 1 Tbs tomato purée.

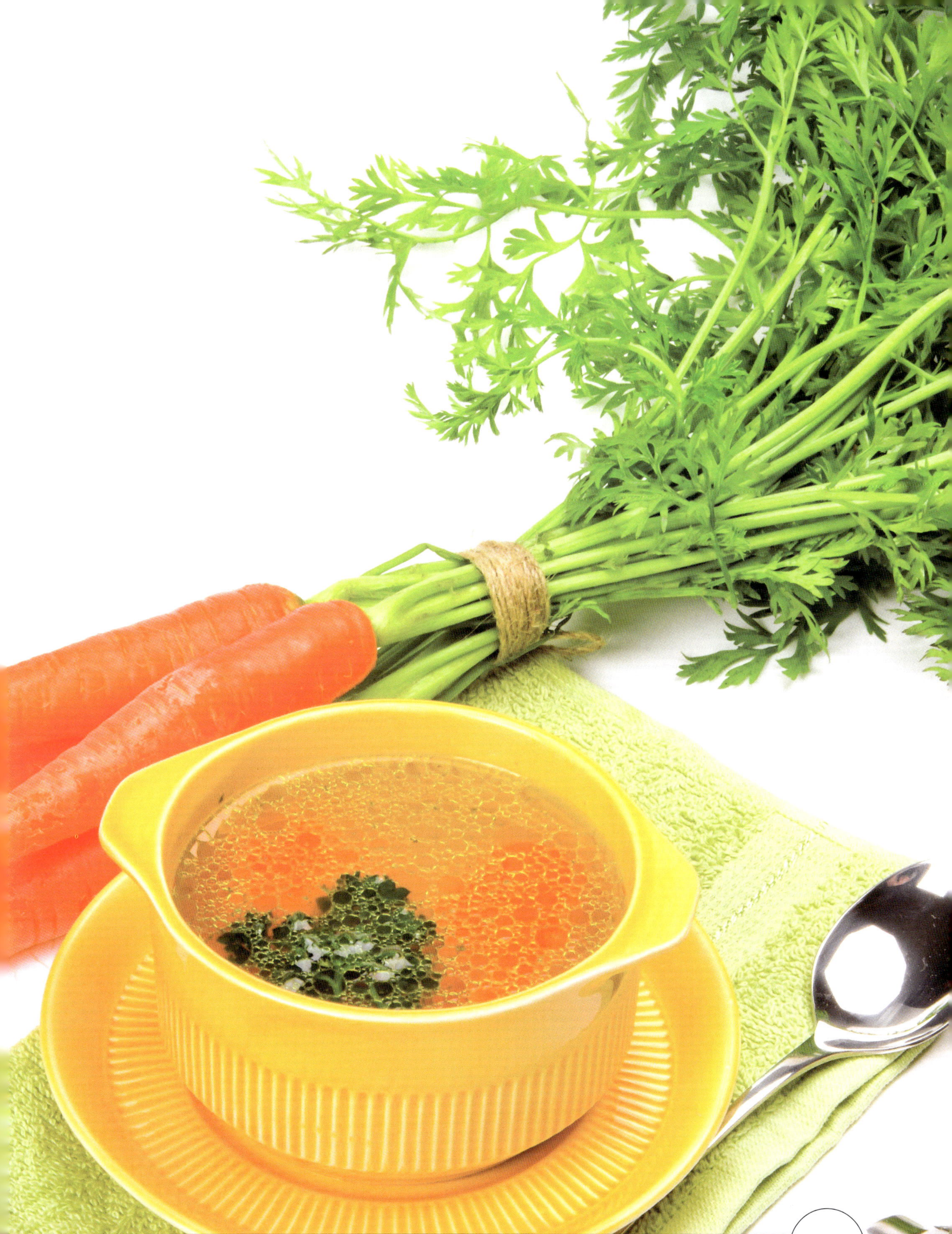

54

Lentil soup

- This is quick and easy and very popular. Start with the usual onion, celery and garlic sautéed together with 1 Tbs each of olive oil and water.
- You can add some finely sliced sweet pepper to this; also, sliced carrots. Next add:

1 cup red lentils
¼ cup white easy-cook rice or brown rice flakes
1½ pints (scant 900 ml) boiling water

- Simmer until cooked – about half an hour.
- Season with herb salt or vegetable stock cube.
- Sprinkle with fresh chopped or freeze-dried parsley.

Variations
Lentil and potato – omit the rice and add 2 cupfuls of chopped potato.
Cabbage – add several cups of finely chopped or shredded cabbage.
Cauliflower – add several cups of finely chopped cauliflower.
Tomato – add a 10-oz tin of chopped tomatoes or ¼ cup tomato paste.

Seasoning variations
Bouquet garni, oregano and fresh coriander are all very good with this soup, as are ground coriander and cumin, and sweet Hungarian paprika.

Carrot and sweet potato soup

This can also be made according to the super-quick method with cashews (see p. 60) or the traditional method with olive oil, which is the one given here.

1 medium-sized sweet potato (orange-coloured flesh)
2 medium-sized carrots
1 large onion
2 Tbs olive oil
1 small orange, peeled
Seasoning

- Roughly chop the onion and sauté in the olive oil until it is soft and transparent.
- Add the carrots and sweet potatoes, cut into chunks, and enough boiling water to just cover them.
- Simmer gently until they are cooked, then allow to cool a little before transferring to the blender.
- Add the orange and seasoning and blend until smooth.
- Sprinkle with fresh or freeze-dried parsley, and serve with a swirl of soya or cashew cream.

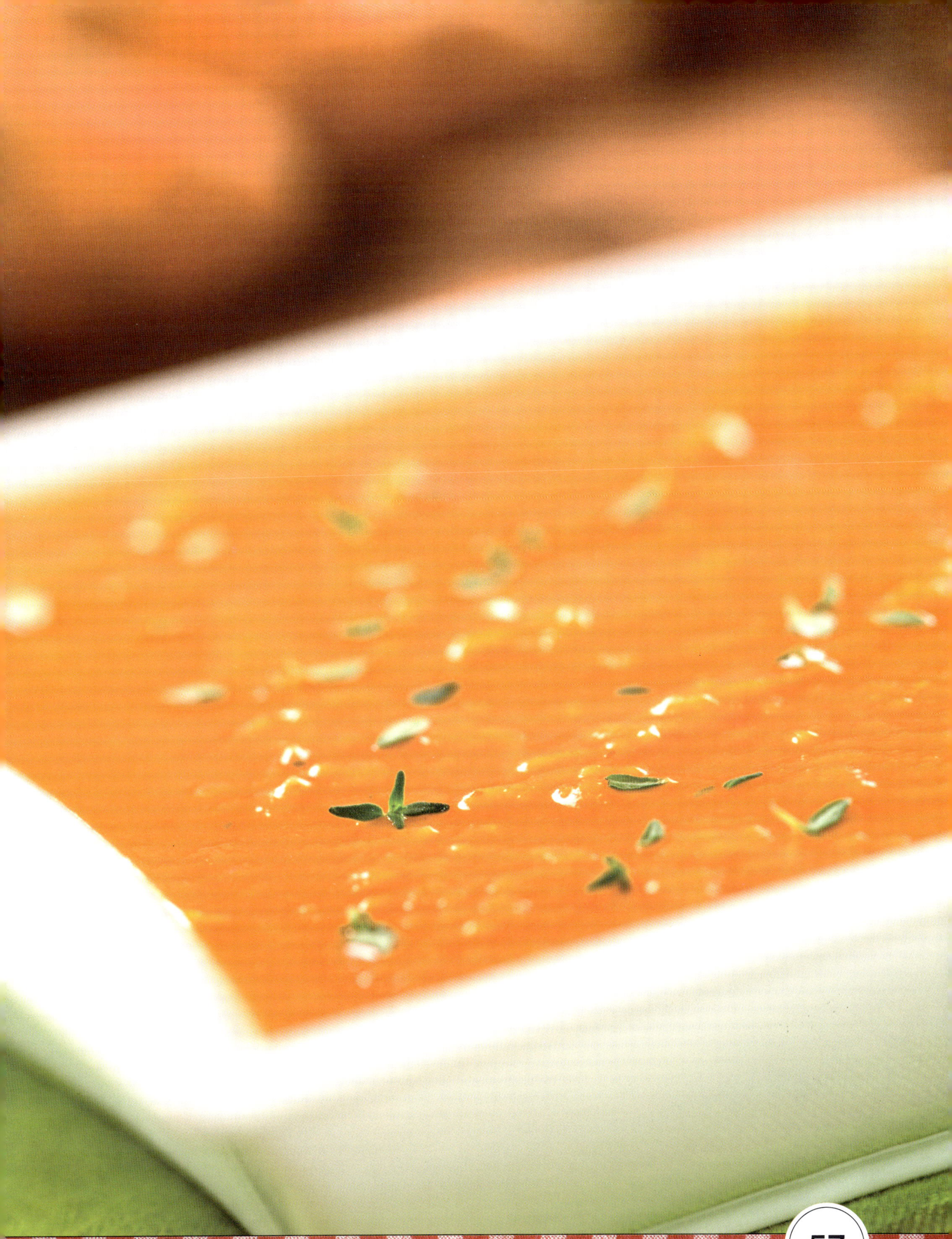

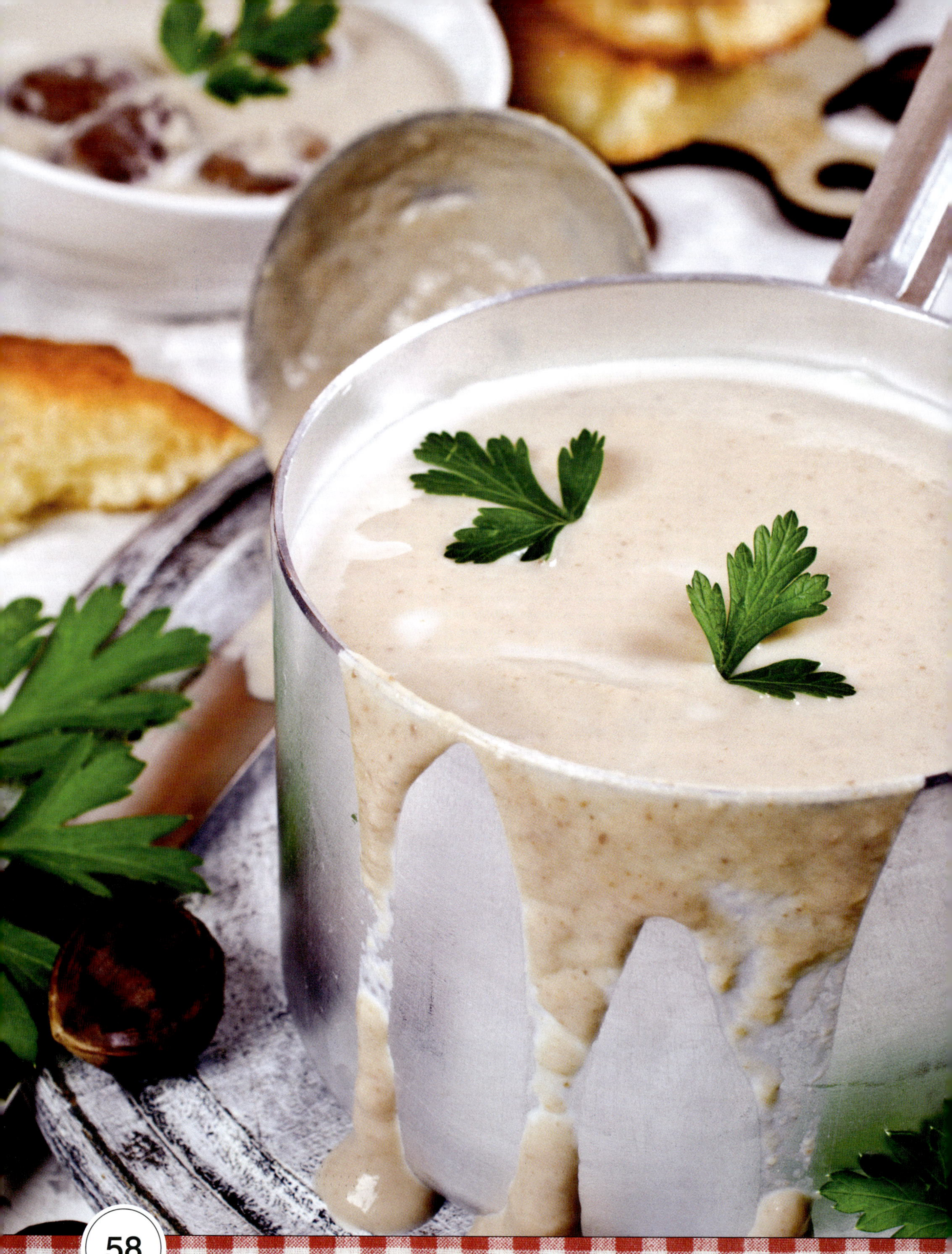

Chestnut soup

1 tin chestnut purée
1 medium-sized onion
1 stick celery
1 clove garlic
1 pint (scant 600ml) water
2 Tbs yeast extract, or your choice of seasoning

Super-quick method
(Smooth soup) Blend everything together until smooth; bring to the boil, stirring; then simmer for 10 minutes or longer. Serve with a swirl of cashew or other non-dairy cream.

Standard method
(Textured soup) Finely chop the onion and celery, crush the garlic, and sauté them in a little olive oil and water. When they are soft, add the chestnut purée, diluted with the water, and the seasoning. Bring gently to the boil and serve with a swirl of non-dairy cream.

Quick and easy spicy parsnip soup

2 medium-sized parsnips
1 medium-sized carrot
1 medium-sized onion
1 stick celery
1 clove garlic
¼ cup cashews or 2 Tbs olive oil
Seasoning – vegetable stock, mild curry powder to taste

Super-quick method with cashews
Cut everything up in chunks, add enough boiling water to cover, and simmer gently for 15-20 minutes. Blend until smooth with mild curry powder or other seasoning, such as coriander or cumin.

Traditional method with olive oil
Sauté the roughly chopped onion, celery and garlic in 2 Tbs olive oil and 1 Tbs water until they are soft and transparent, then add the roughly cut parsnips and carrots with enough boiling water to cover them, simmer gently for 15-20 minutes, then season and blend thoroughly.

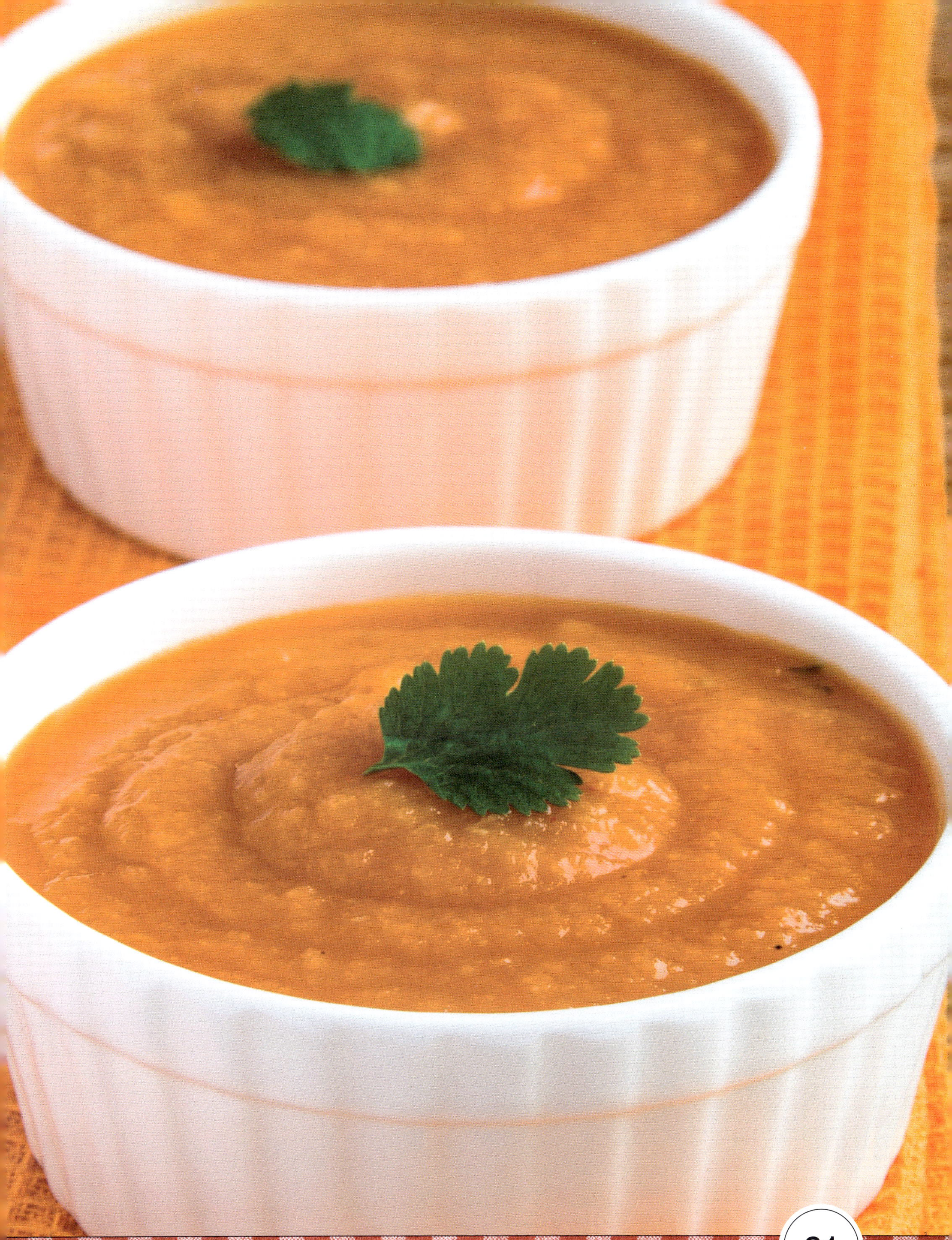

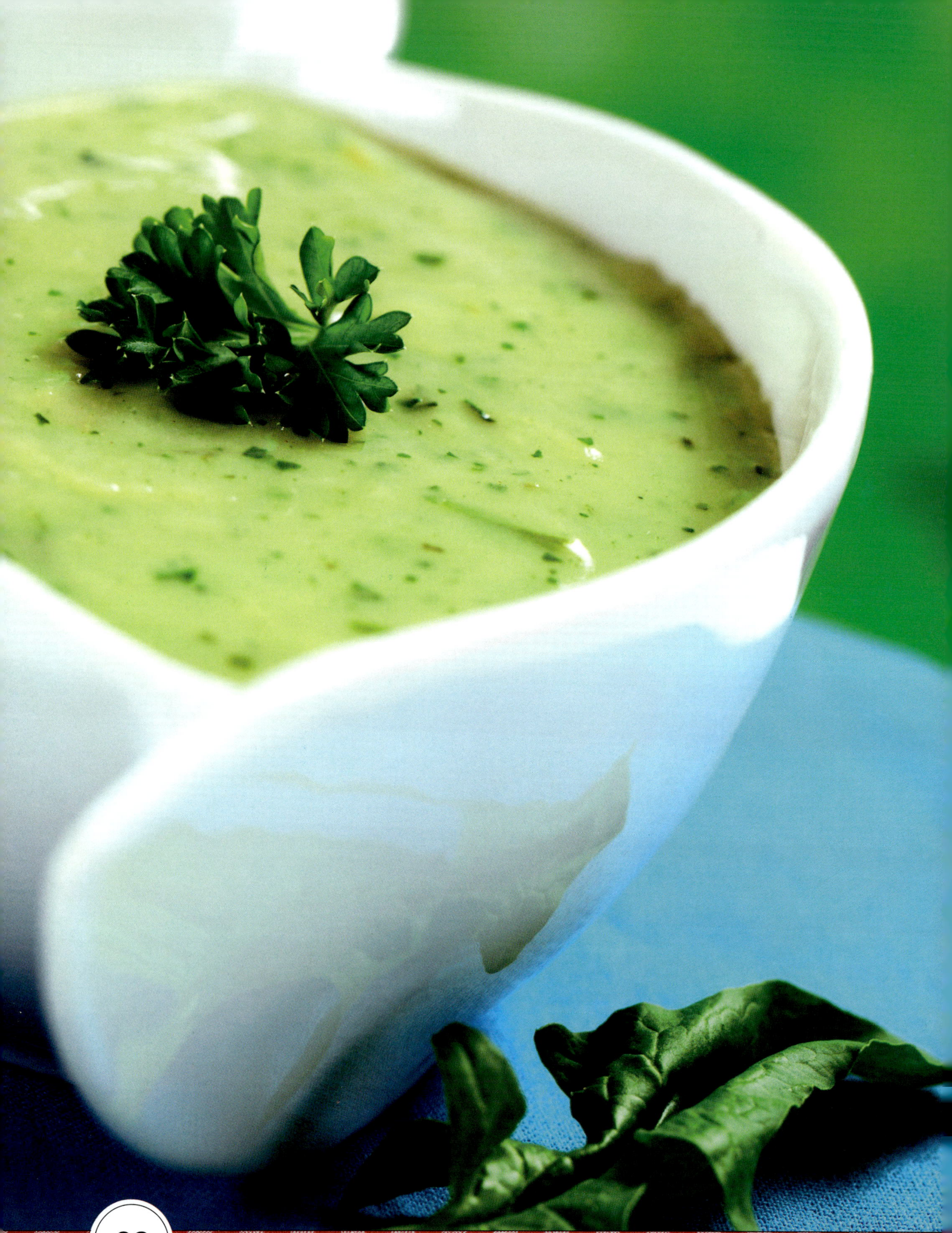

Healthy spinach soup

500g leaf or beet spinach, washed
100g cashew nuts
2 small spring onions, washed
1 small onion, washed
1 tsp fresh or ground ginger
3 medium-sized cloves garlic
Salt to taste
½ teaspoon cumin
Pinch of cayenne pepper (if desired)
1 ½ cups water

- Bring water to boil, and add spinach.
- Liquidise spinach, together with leftover water and all other ingredients, and then serve.

CREAM SOUPS

Creamed corn soup

Dairy-free cream soups can be made with cashew or sunflower cream. Super-easy cream soup is made by cooking everything in the saucepan together, letting it cool briefly, then blending. For a cream soup with more texture, the cream is made separately and added when the vegetables have cooked. Cashews make the smoothest, richest cream, but sunflower seeds are good too, and are much cheaper; or use a mixture of the two.

1 medium-sized onion
1 stick celery
1 medium carrot
1 medium potato
1 tin sweetcorn
⅓ cup cashew nuts (or sunflower seeds, or a mixture)
Seasoning

- Chop or dice the vegetables and cook in just enough water to cover.
- When cooked, add ½ tin sweetcorn.
- Blend the rest of the sweetcorn with the cashews or sunflower seeds with just enough water to cover them.
- When smooth, add to the soup.
- Add seasoning and chopped parsley or fresh coriander, and enough water to bring to the desired consistency.

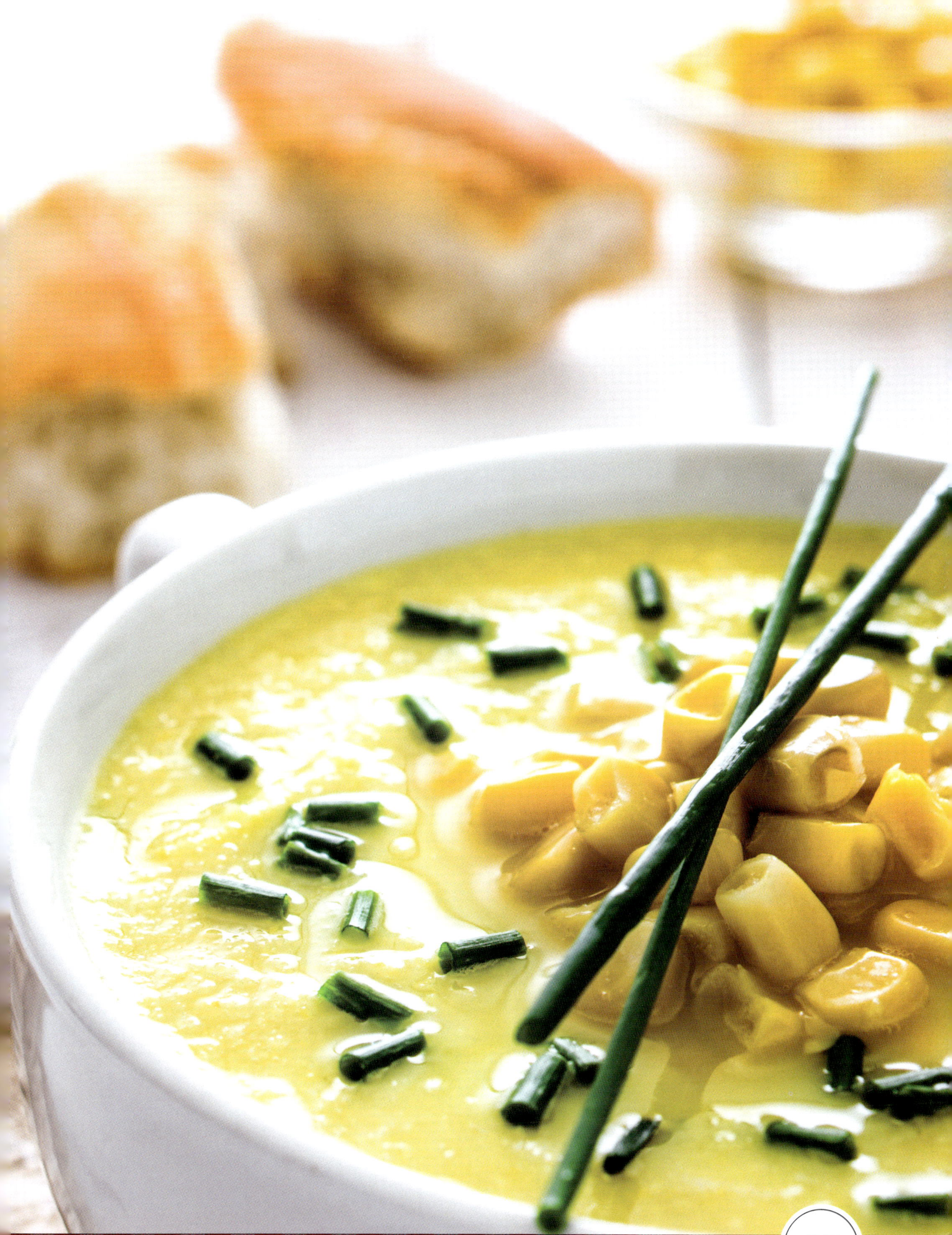

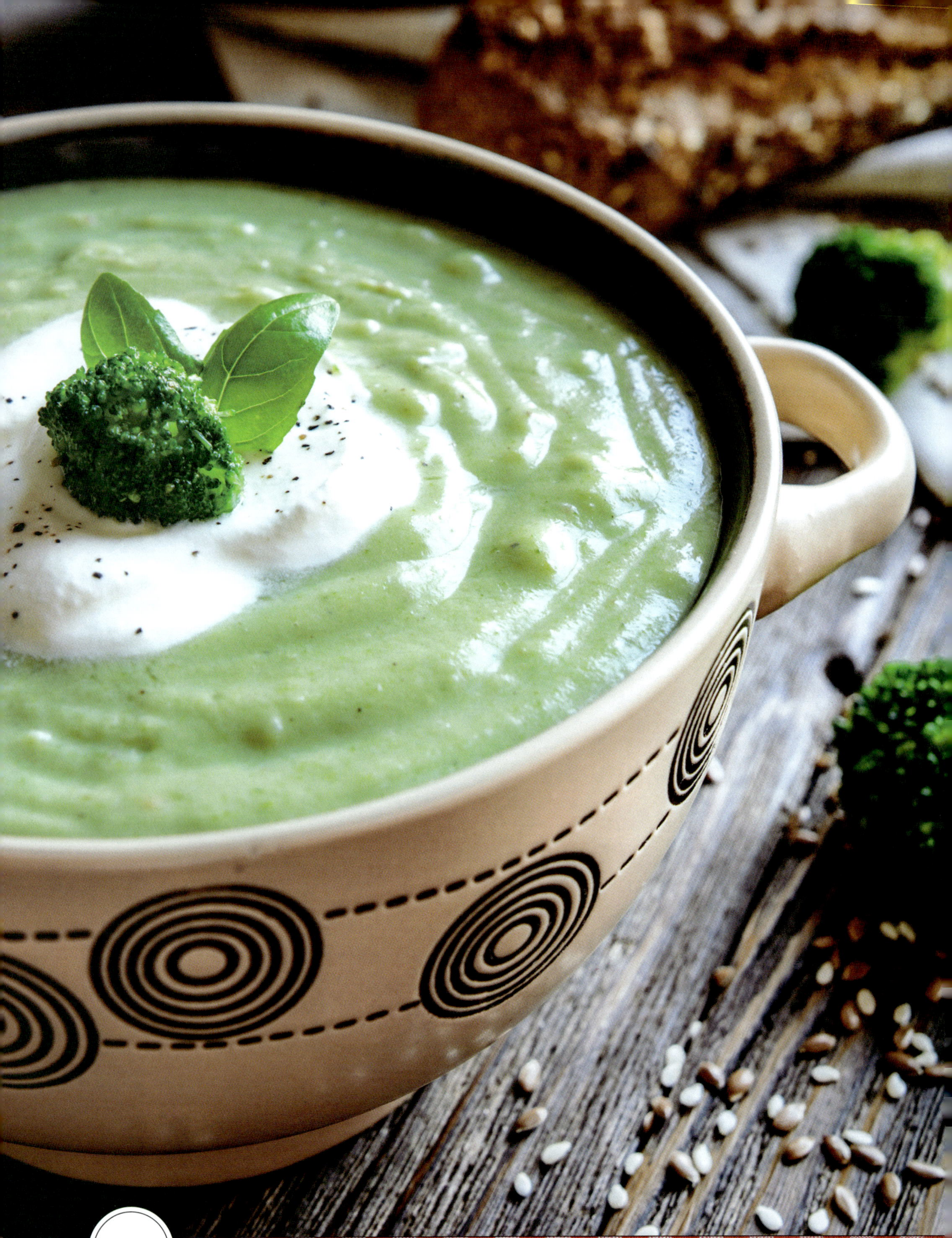

Cream of broccoli stalk soup

This may sound rather frugal, but it tastes good.

1 medium-sized onion
1 stick celery
1 clove garlic
2 thick broccoli stalks
⅓ cup cashew nuts or sunflower seeds, or a mixture of both
1 vegetable stock cube or other seasoning

- Cut the onion, celery and broccoli stalks into a few pieces, put in a saucepan with the cashews or seeds and the garlic, and add 1 pint or a generous ½ litre boiling water.
- Cover and cook for 15-20 minutes.
- Allow to cool a little, then blend until smooth. Add more water if desired.
- Garnish with parsley or fresh chives. For a thicker soup, add a chopped potato or ¼ cup easy-cook rice before cooking, or add some leftover cooked rice or other cereal before blending.

Mixed vegetable cream soup

This soup is not blended, so there is a little chopping to do.

1 medium onion, chopped
1 celery stick, thinly sliced
1 large carrot, thinly sliced or diced
1 potato, chopped in larger pieces than the carrot
1 clove garlic, crushed
1½ pints (scant 900ml) boiling water

- Cover the pan, and simmer until the vegetables are almost cooked, then add ½ cup frozen peas.
- Add ½ cup blended cashews (or sunflower seeds, or mixture), seasoning (salt) and, just before serving, chopped parsley or chives.

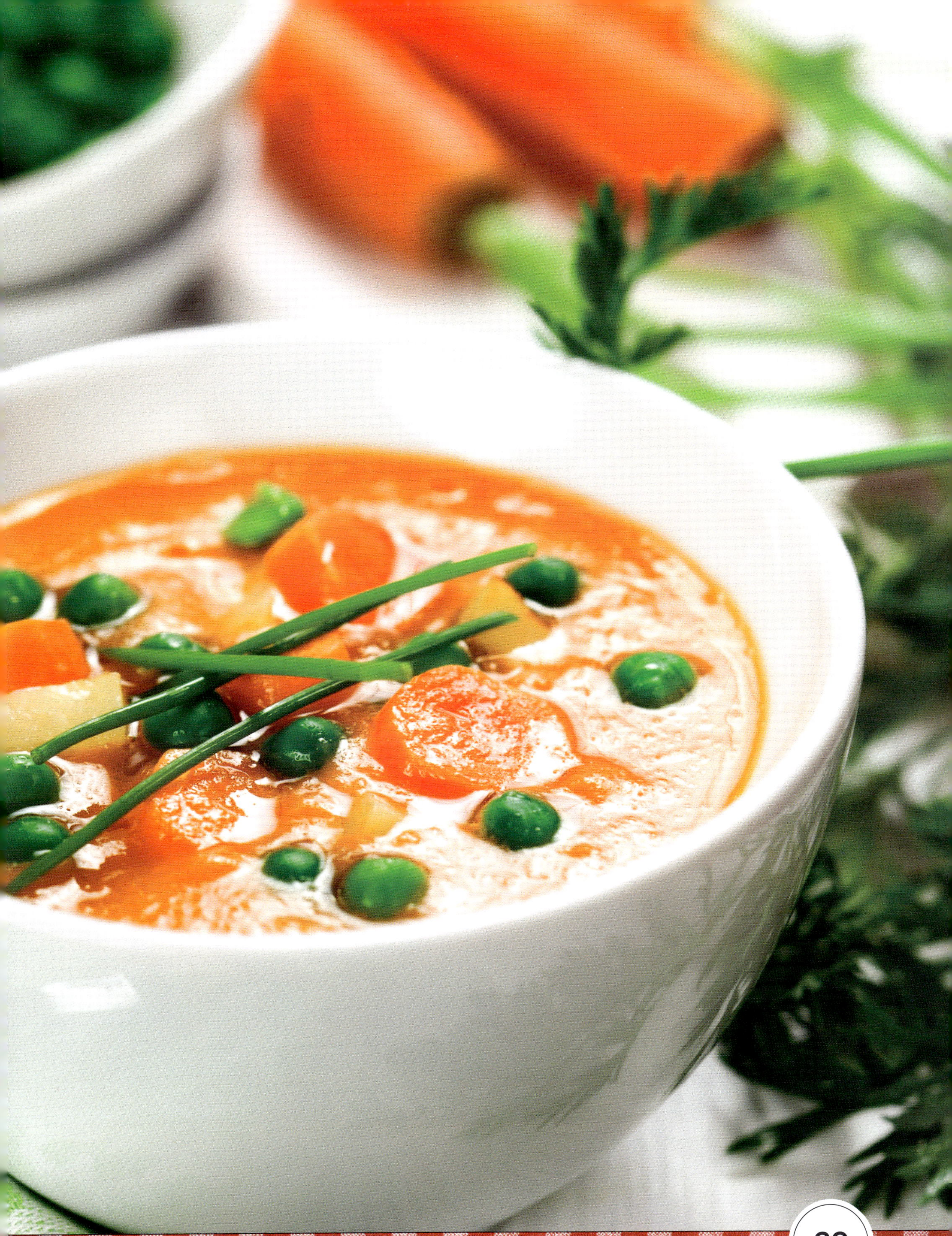

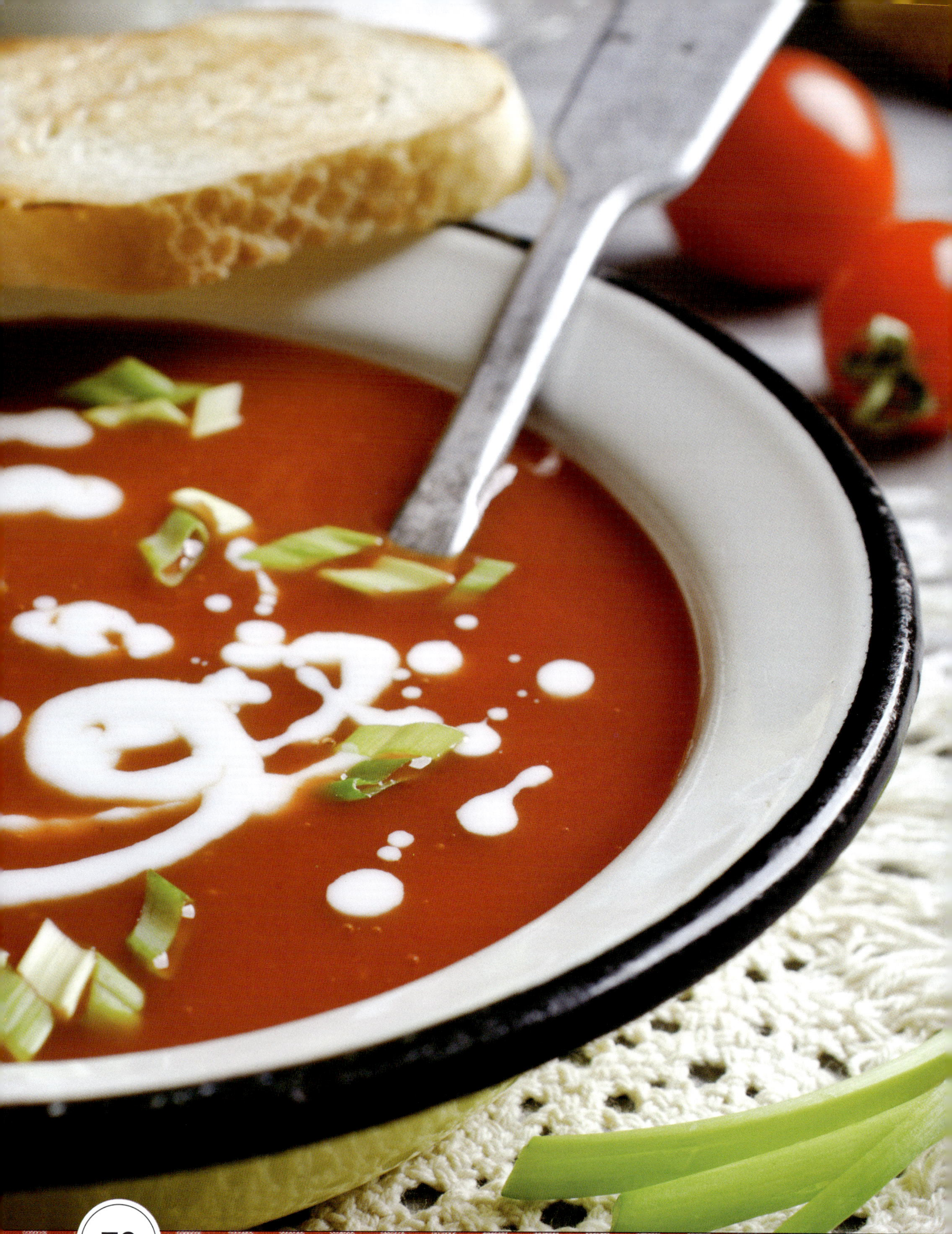

Tomato cream soup

1 medium-sized onion, roughly chopped
1 stick celery, roughly chopped
1 clove garlic
⅓ cup cashews or sunflower seeds
1 (10-oz) tin tomatoes in juice with equal volume of water
2 Tbs tomato paste
1 vegetable stock cube or your choice of seasoning
Basil or parsley

- Cook everything together for 10-15 minutes, then blend until smooth.
- Add fresh parsley leaves a few seconds before you stop the blender.
- Add fresh basil leaves just before serving.

Pumpkin soup

1 medium-sized pumpkin, finely chopped
½ small onion, sliced
2 cloves garlic, crushed
¼ tsp thyme
1 large peeled carrot, finely chopped
¼ tsp cayenne pepper
1 large potato
Slice of yam
1 green banana
1 tania (Caribbean root vegetable)
1 spring onion
½ cup each of green, yellow and red pepper slices
1 small tin coconut milk
1 vegetable stock cube
4 cups water

- Pour water in saucepan and add salt.
- Bring to boil and add pumpkin, garlic, onion and peppers, until soft and mushy.
- Add the rest of the ingredients and bring to boil; then simmer until all vegetables are cooked.
- Add more hot water, if necessary, for consistency.
  - **Optional:** if you like, add dumplings and cook for a further 5 minutes.

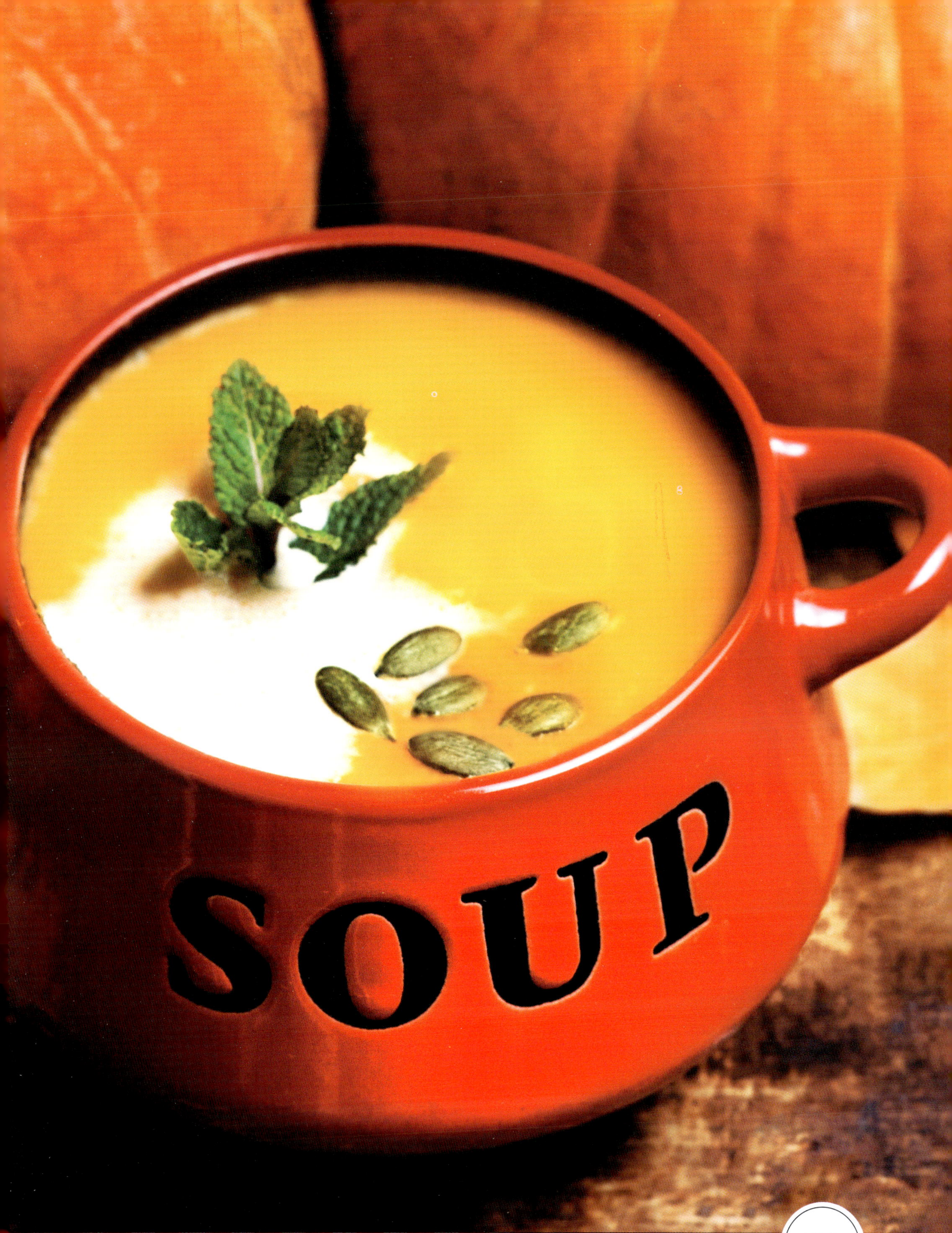
SOUP

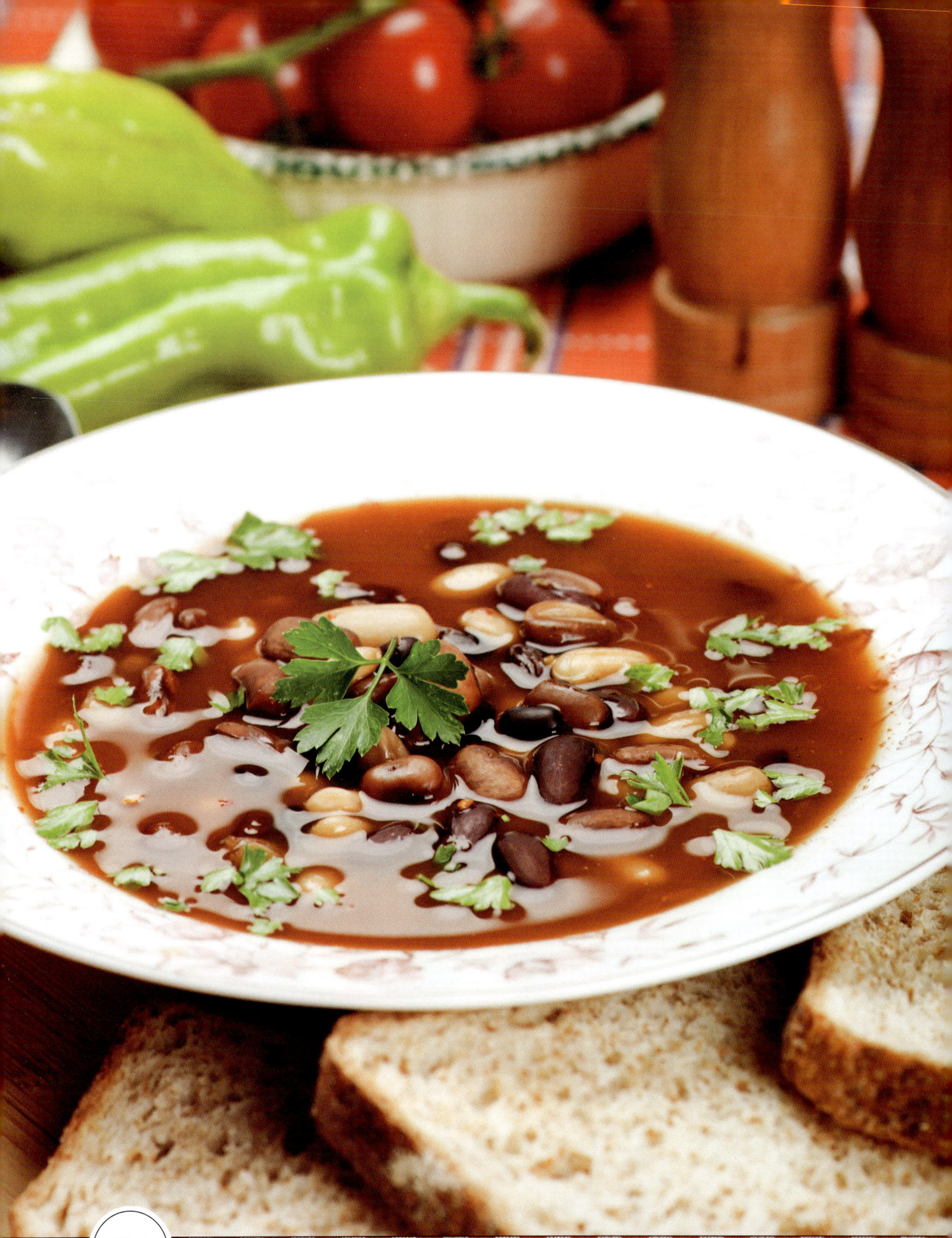

Balkan bean soup

BEAN SOUPS

1 medium-sized onion, chopped
1 small red or green pepper, chopped
1 clove garlic, crushed
1 tsp sweet Hungarian paprika
1 medium-sized carrot, thinly sliced
1 medium-sized potato, thickly sliced
1½ cups cooked red kidney beans
Herb salt to taste

- Sauté the first three ingredients in a little olive oil, or oil and water, or water.
- Add the carrot, potato and beans, and enough boiling water to cover them.
- Simmer until the vegetables are cooked, then stir in paprika and herb salt to taste.

These are nourishing, filling soups. Served with wholemeal bread or crispbread and a large salad, they provide an appetising, balanced and nutritious meal.

Minestrone

1 medium-sized onion, chopped
1 medium-sized carrot, diced
1 medium-sized potato, diced
1 stick celery, chopped
Other vegetables, such as courgettes, cauliflower, cabbage, cut in small pieces
¼ cup easy-cook rice or ½ cup cooked rice
1½ cups cooked haricot beans
1 clove garlic, crushed
Seasonings – herb salt, oregano or other herbs

- Sauté the onion, celery and garlic, then add the other vegetables and enough boiling water to cover generously.
- Add the rice and seasonings, and lastly the cooked beans.
- Simmer until the vegetables are cooked, and garnish with some chopped fresh parsley.

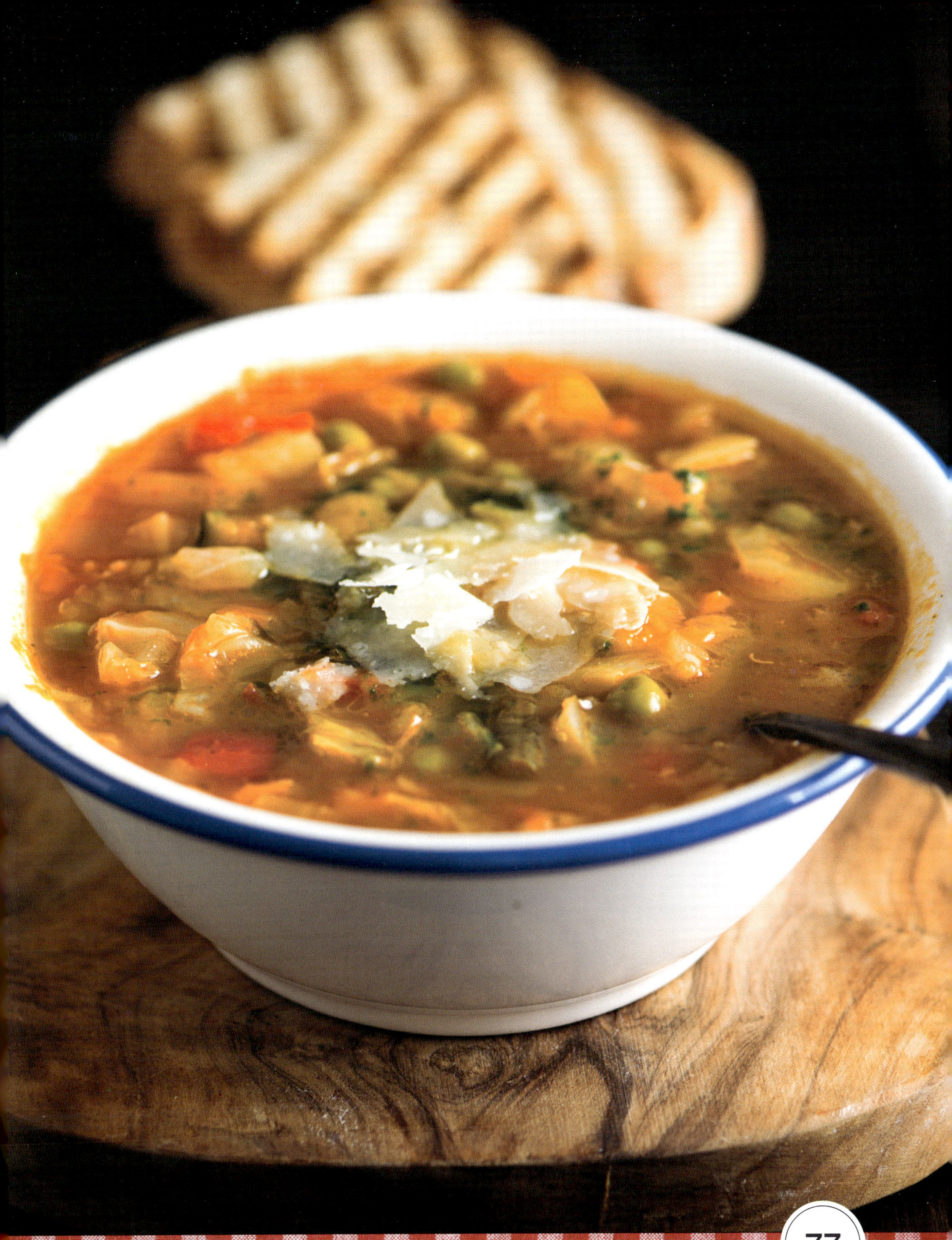

78

Potage crème d'haricots

1 medium-sized onion
1 stick celery
1 clove garlic
½ sweet red pepper
Olive oil
1½ cups cooked haricot beans
Water or soya milk

- Sauté the onion, celery, garlic and sweet pepper together.
- Blend with the haricot beans and add soya milk or water to bring it to the desired consistency.
- Season well with fresh parsley, fresh coriander, chopped fresh chives, herb salt or other vegetable seasoning.
- Serve with a sprinkle of paprika.

TO EAT WITH SOUP

Sometimes we like our soups to have a little something extra.

Sunflower or cashew cream
½ cup sunflower seeds or cashew nuts, or a mixture of both

- Add just enough water to cover the seeds and allow the blender blades to turn easily. Blend until smooth.
- For a thinner cream, add extra water at the end.

Sunflower or cashew sour cream
- As above, adding 2 Tbs lemon juice and ½ tsp herbs after blending.

Garlic sour cream
- Make the above recipe, adding a small clove of fresh garlic, ¼ tsp garlic powder or garlic purée to taste before blending.

Croutons
- Cut 4-5 slices of bread into small cubes, sprinkle with a little water and toss in a mixture of ¼ tsp herb salt, ½ tsp garlic powder and 1 Tbs dried mixed herbs until thoroughly mixed.
- Spread on a baking tray and cook in a moderately hot oven until crisp and golden.

Crispy crackers
1 cup wholewheat flour
1 cup porridge oats
⅓ cup olive oil
½ cup water
Pinch of salt

- Mix well, roll out thinly, cut into strips or squares and bake in a moderately hot oven until crisp and golden – about 10 minutes.
- Cool on a wire rack.

100% whole-food crackers
1 cup wholewheat flour
1 cup porridge oats
1 cup sunflower seeds, ground in coffee mill
½ cup or more of water
Pinch of salt
½ tsp each of ground coriander and cumin

- Mix everything together to a fairly stiff dough. Roll out and bake as for crispy crackers.

81

SALADS

Introduction

Something raw at every meal is a good motto and one that gives salad a major role in our diets. Here are some salad suggestions, some plant-based alternatives to mayonnaise, and a vinegar-free alternative to vinaigrette.

If you want to fill up on highly nutritious low-calorie foods and leave less room for other things, a big salad is the ideal way to start a meal.

Choose a wide variety of vegetables.
These salad recipes are very flexible. Most vegetables can be eaten raw, so the possible variations are enormous.

Although most people could eat much more raw food than they do, we don't recommend that you eat all your vegetables raw, as some nutrients are more easily absorbed after cooking. Choose a selection each day, some raw and some cooked, from the wide variety of vegetables that are available now.

SALAD RECIPES
A SELECTION OF RAW SALADS

Simple salads consisting of one vegetable with one herb and a little dressing are quick and easy to make and delicious.

Tomato salad
- Slice tomatoes thinly, arrange on a plate and sprinkle with French dressing and herbs.
- Fresh basil goes wonderfully with tomatoes: just tear up a few leaves and sprinkle them on the salad.

Carrot salad
- Finely grate carrot, and sprinkle with lemon juice and chopped fresh dill or parsley.

Sweet pepper salad
- Slice sweet peppers thinly, and sprinkle with salt and olive oil.

Cucumber salad
- For 1 cup cucumber cut in very thin slices or small cubes (1cm or less), add 1 Tbs French dressing and ½ Tbs chopped fresh dill, or ¼ Tbs freeze-dried dill, and mix gently.

Tossed salad
- The classic tossed salad is lettuce or other green leaves with a French dressing.
- Sliced tomato and cucumber, finely sliced onions and chopped chives are good additions, while for a dark-green colour contrast, use some chopped parsley, watercress, rocket or baby spinach.
- Sliced avocado is good too, and when good tomatoes are hard to find, or very expensive, try thinly sliced orange instead.

Winter salad
- A classic winter salad can be made up of grated carrot and finely shredded white cabbage with French dressing or mayonnaise.
- Add chopped parsley, chives, dill or other fresh green herbs for colour and flavour, finely chopped onion for added taste, grated swede for a tang, or grated apple for a sweet or tart contrast.

Green, white and orange salad
½ head of Chinese leaf, sliced fairly finely
1 orange, peeled and chopped
Small bunch of dark green leaves such as watercress, rocket, roughly chopped baby spinach or finely chopped parsley.

- Mix with 2 tsp olive oil and herb salt to taste.

Carrot and celeriac salad
Grate equal quantities of carrot and celeriac and mix together, then add your choice of dressing – French, mayonnaise, or simply lemon juice and salt. This is extra good with toasted sunflower and pumpkin seeds sprinkled on top.

Raw beetroot salad
- Mix finely grated raw beetroot with equal parts grated carrot and apple.
- Sprinkle with lemon juice and herb salt, or mix with French dressing or mayonnaise, or a mixture of both.

Some other additions to raw salads
Sprouted seeds: Mung bean shoots and sprouted alfalfa seeds are probably the best-known. However, apart from bean shoots, it's not always easy to find them, so if you like them then sprout your own. Sprouted seeds are delicious and very nutritious, too. As the seeds sprout, they develop vitamin C and become more digestible. You can mix them into salads or eat them on their own.

Tinned foods: Artichoke hearts – marinate them in citronette; palm hearts, water chestnuts, asparagus spears, corn, beans and chickpeas are all useful ingredients.

Sprinkle toppings
Seeds: Sunflower and pumpkin – can be toasted first.

Nuts: For example, chopped or ground walnuts, flaked almonds, cashew pieces.

Sun-dried tomatoes, chopped or sliced.

Olives soothe the digestive system and can be eaten with almost any kind of salad, served separately or mixed in.
   A couple of suggestions: cut pitted green olives into a grated carrot salad, and black Greek olives into a tossed salad.

Fruit in salads: Sharp fruits in small amounts go well with vegetable salads – chopped orange, small pineapple chunks, tart apples, etc. Dried fruits such as raisins, sultanas and chopped dried apricots, in small amounts, can liven up winter salads.

COOKED VEGETABLE SALADS

Potato salad
- Waxy potatoes are best, preferably steamed and then peeled.
- Use either French or mayonnaise-type dressings. Chopped onions, chives or other fresh herbs make good additions.

Russian salad
- This is a potato salad with cooked diced carrots and green peas in a mayonnaise dressing.

Beetroot salad
- Dice cooked beetroot into small cubes and sprinkle with lemon juice and salt.

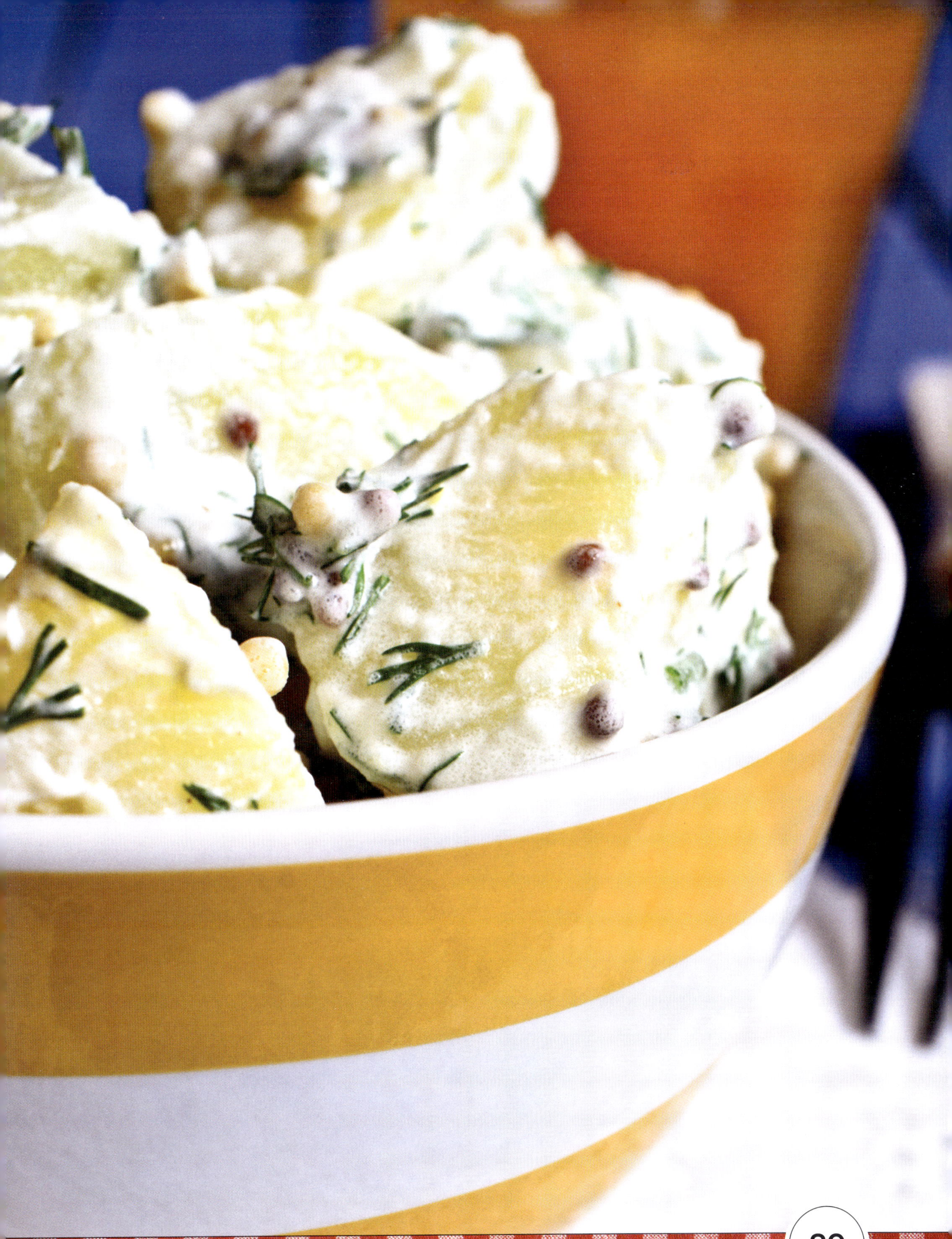

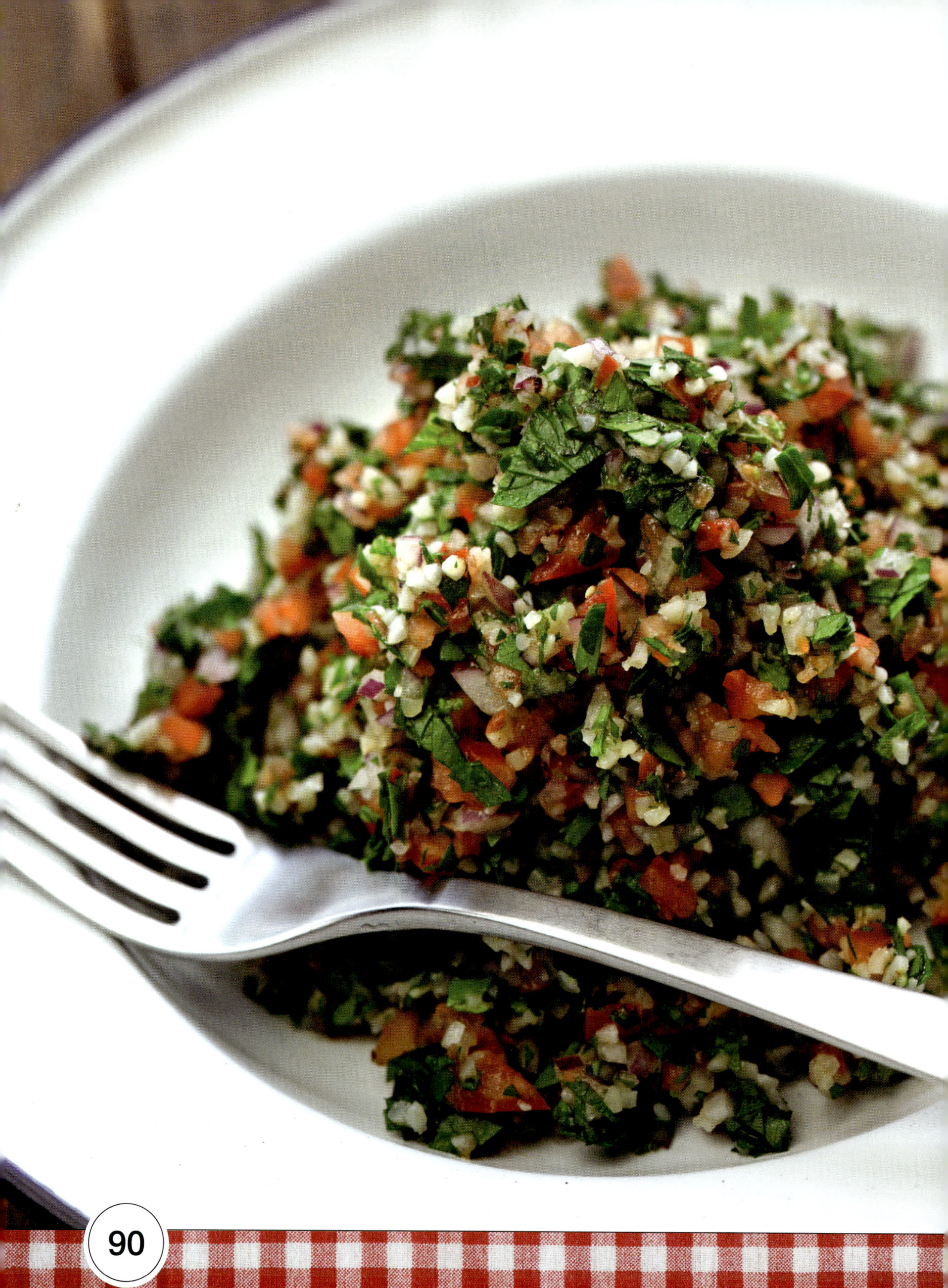

Rice salad

2 cups cooked brown rice
2 Tbs cashew pieces
1 Tbs sultanas
¼ cup finely sliced celery
½ cup diced cucumber

- Mix it together with 2 Tbs French dressing and fresh or dried parsley.

Corn salad

1 medium-sized tin sweetcorn, drained
1 small onion, finely chopped
Sweet pepper, small piece, chopped
2 sun-dried tomatoes, cut in small strips
1 Tbs parsley, chopped

- Mix together with French dressing or mayonnaise.

Tabouli

This is a Middle Eastern dish, based on cooked wheat, but with lots of raw things, too.

½ cup cracked wheat
¼ cup fresh parsley, finely chopped
⅓ cup spring onions, chopped
½ cup cucumber, chopped
1½ cups tomato, chopped
1 clove garlic, crushed
2 Tbs lemon juice
1 Tbs fresh mint, chopped
2 Tbs parsley, chopped (optional)
Salt or herb salt to taste

- Put the cracked wheat in a pan with 1 cup water, and cook gently until all the water is absorbed (about 15 minutes).
- When cool, add all the other ingredients and mix together well.

Bean salad

- Mix any selection of cooked beans with citronette dressing.

STARCH-BASED SALADS

Corn, rice, beans and pasta are often used as salads, too. These are more like cold main dishes, because the amounts of fresh and raw materials are usually quite small. They are a useful form of filling food for hot days.

Add small, crisp, colourful and flavourful items, mainly raw, to your basic ingredient in whatever proportions you like and add your choice of dressing.

SALAD DRESSINGS

Salad dressings are important. They can be as simple as a sprinkling of lemon juice and/or olive oil and salt.

Lemon juice aids digestion and oil facilitates the absorption of the fat-soluble vitamins in your salads, so, unless you have specific health problems, don't hesitate to use an oil-and-lemon dressing (in moderation). These dressings are not limited to salads, either: they are very good on baked potatoes and other cooked vegetables.

The mayonnaise recipes are for family-size quantities, and should keep for 1½-2 weeks in the fridge.

Tofu mayonnaise (oil-free)
1 250g pack tofu
½ cup cashews blended smooth in just enough water to cover
2-3 Tbs lemon juice
1 Tbs garlic purée
Herb salt to taste

- Crumble the tofu and add to the blender with the other ingredients and enough soya milk or water to enable the blender blades to turn easily.
- Blend together briefly. Option – add a handful of fresh parsley with the tofu and other ingredients.

Soya mayonnaise (definitely not oil-free, so not for serious weight-reducing diets)

1 cup soya milk
1 cup oil (light olive oil works well)
2-3 Tbs lemon juice
Seasoning – herb salt, garlic powder, etc.

Everything should be at room temperature.
- Blend the oil and soya milk for about a minute, transfer to a bowl, add the seasonings, then *very gently fold (do not stir)* in the lemon juice, which will cause the mixture to thicken and it will thicken further as it stands.

Citronette French dressing
1 Tbs lemon juice
2 Tbs olive oil
1 Tbs yeast flakes (optional)
½ tsp herb salt (or to taste)
1 tsp garlic purée (optional)

- Put everything in a jar with a tightly fitting lid, and shake vigorously until thoroughly mixed.

This can be used on cooked vegetables, as well as salad, and is excellent with baked potatoes. It keeps well in the fridge for several weeks.

Oil-free citronette
- Make exactly as for standard citronette, replacing the oil with soya or any other non-dairy milk.

Sunflower cashew cream
½ cup sunflower seeds or cashew nuts or a mixture of the two

- Add just enough water to cover them and allow the blender blades to turn easily. Blend until smooth.
- For a thinner cream, add extra water at the end.

Vegan sour cream
½ cup sunflower seeds or cashew nuts or a mixture of the two
2 Tbs lemon juice
½ tsp herb salt

- Make as for the above recipe, adding lemon juice and salt after blending.

Garlic 'cream' dressing
Make the above recipe, adding a small clove of fresh garlic, ¼ tsp garlic powder or ½ tsp garlic purée before blending.

94

Hummus

1 tin chickpeas (1½ cups)
⅓ cup tahini
1 small onion
1 clove garlic
3-5 Tbs lemon juice

- Blend, adding just enough water to allow blades to turn.
- Add salt to taste, and 2-3 Tbs olive oil if desired.
- Optional extras – add some chopped fresh red pepper, sweet paprika powder or fresh herbs to the mixture in the blender.

Guacamole

This Mexican avocado side dish is a very good dip or spread.
- One way of making it is to mash a medium-sized avocado with 1 Tbs of any of the aforementioned salad dressings.
- Add extra lemon juice, salt and garlic to taste.
- You can also add a finely chopped tomato and some very finely chopped or grated onion.

Tofu dips

- All sorts of tasty dips can be made from tofu. Simply mash a block of tofu, with enough soya milk, soya mayonnaise or other salad dressing to give the desired consistency.
- Add whatever colourful or flavourful things you like, such as finely chopped onion, garlic, sweet pepper, parsley, coriander or dill, and add herb salt to taste.

Tofu cottage 'cheese'

1 250g pack tofu, mashed
1 tsp garlic purée
1 tsp tarragon or other dried herbs
Salt or herb salt to taste
Lemon juice to taste
Soya milk, non-dairy cream or mayonnaise

- Mix together, adding enough nut or soya milk, cream or mayonnaise to make it hold together.

CRUDITÉS AND DIPS

Crudités are fresh raw vegetables cut in strips or small pieces, served with one or more thick dressings into which they can be dipped.

Popular vegetables are carrots, courgettes, celery, cucumber, peppers, tomato wedges, broccoli and cauliflower florets, crisp small lettuce leaves and radishes.

Tofu mayonnaise, soya mayonnaise, hummus and tofu cottage cheese blended with some extra soya milk all make good dips.

These dips are also good as side dishes to eat with other salads.

MAIN MEALS

Introduction

The use of the terms 'main course' or 'main meal', when referring to meals, implies that this particular part of the meal is being preceded and/or followed by other courses. A simple example of this would be a serving of a soup before the main course and a serving of dessert afterwards. At the heart of the main meal there is traditionally a serving of protein (such as beef, lamb, chicken, pork or fish), while for the vegetarian or vegan alternative one must expect a plant-based substitute.

The meals that will follow in this section are quite capable of standing alone as the only selection or combination of food to be presented at the family dinner table during the chief meal of the day. They may also be grouped with recipes from the soup and dessert sections of this book when more elaborate dining is required.

Nuts

Nuts are delicious, nourishing and rich. Their hard shells and the work necessary to reach them suggest that it is best to eat them in small quantities – the amount that you might eat if you had to shell them for yourself. Another guideline is that the harder the shell, the richer the nut is likely to be, and the smaller the amount necessary to satisfy.

Nuts are rich in fat and protein. They contain many other nutrients and add interest, variety and even luxury to plant-food diets. Nuts are easy to use and versatile, useful for sweet or savoury recipes.

Buying and storing nuts: the shells are the natural means of preserving and protecting nuts, so unshelled nuts are the easiest to store, and will normally remain good from one season to the next. Shelled nuts will not keep so well. Being high in fat they have a tendency to go rancid. Nuts are one of the more expensive types of raw material in a plant-based diet. They are, however, much cheaper when bought in bulk. Keeping them fresh is not a problem if you have a freezer: use it for long-term storage of all shelled nuts and use your fridge for short-term storage.

Turn to page 110 for some tasty variations on how to make a nut roast.

Some tips for those who find nuts hard to digest:
- Chew them well.
- Reduce the amount of nuts in the recipe – or increase the amount of starch.
- Substitute beans, lentils or seeds for some of the nuts in the recipe.
- Keep the menu simple when nut foods are on it.

Beans

Beans are a nutritious, economical class of food, a rich source of carbohydrate, protein, fibre and other essential nutrients, including phytochemicals that promote health and longevity. Beans must be thoroughly cooked for the body to get the full benefit of these nutrients and to avoid the well-known digestive problems that beans can cause. For most people beans are not nearly as indigestible as some would have us believe. Most bean problems can be avoided by adequate cooking, adequate chewing, avoiding too many different types of food at the same meal as the beans, and not eating between meals.

   Baked beans are one of the most popular tinned foods, and they are very convenient and useful; but most brands contain a lot of sugar, so choose carefully if you are going to use them often.

Planning bean meals:

Beans are a concentrated high-protein plant food, so keep the rest of the meal simple. Serve plenty of vegetables, at least some of them as a fresh raw salad, and some potatoes, wholegrain bread or other starchy food.

Quantities for beans

1 cup dried beans yields 2 cups cooked beans.
1 tin cooked beans or chickpeas usually contains about 1 cupful.

Before cooking:

Rinse the beans well, then soak overnight or for at least eight hours in plenty of water. Before cooking drain off the water, rinse again and add enough fresh water to cover generously. Extra soaked beans can be frozen in convenient quantities to use later. Freezing also reduces cooking time.

Cooking methods:

Bring to the boil and simmer until beans are tender.

Pressure cook – this is the best method for soya beans and chickpeas. Follow the cooker instructions.
Slow cooker/crockpot – cook according to individual crockpot instructions.

> **Helpful hints:**
> - Flavourings such as bay leaves, caraway or coriander seeds can be cooked with beans.
> - Add the salt after the beans are fully cooked: this shortens the cooking time.
> - Add a squeeze of lemon juice to cooked beans to enhance flavour and aid digestion.
> - If all this is too time-consuming, use tinned beans. Most supermarkets now stock a variety of plain cooked beans, some without added sugar and salt.

Cooking times for beans and other pulses

Soak all except lentils, split peas and mung beans overnight, or for at least 8 hours. Use three or four cups of water for each cup of beans. After soaking, discard the water and rinse well. Add a similar amount of water, bring to the boil and cook until tender and easy to mash with a fork. Times are an approximate guide – some beans may need longer. If more water is needed always top up with boiling water: don't let the beans cool down while cooking as it may cause them to remain hard. Pressure cooking will reduce time by about two thirds.

Haricot and similar-sized beans	2 hours
Red kidney beans	2 to 3 hours
Soya beans	5 hours or more
Chickpeas	3 hours
Split peas	1 hour
Red lentils	40 minutes
Green lentils	1 hour
Mung beans	1 hour

Cooking soya beans

NB: They must be very well cooked.
Soak them for 8 to 24 hours.
Cook them for 5 hours, or 1 to 2 hours in a pressure cooker.
Once they are cooked they can be used as any other type of bean.

Beans and the digestive system

Beans are notorious for causing flatulence (wind). To avoid this problem, be sure the beans are thoroughly cooked, chewed well, and eaten as part of an otherwise simple menu.

MAINS RECIPES
BEANS

Very easy beans

The easiest way to prepare beans is to use tinned beans. If you are in a serious hurry you can omit the sautéed vegetables, simply mixing beans, tomatoes and seasonings. Don't add salt – it comes in the baked beans.

1 tin each of baked beans, haricot beans, red kidney beans, and chickpeas.
1 tin chopped tomatoes and/or 1 to 2 Tbs tomato paste
1 Tbs garlic purée
1 Tbs sweet paprika
1 Tbs oregano or other herbs

- Drain the haricot and other beans and chickpeas and add them to the baked beans and chopped tomatoes.
- Stir in your favourite herbs, e.g. 1 tsp dried oregano, a small bunch of fresh coriander (chopped), or 1 tsp mixed herbs.
- If you have time, chop and sauté an onion, a small pepper and a stick of celery in olive oil and water until it is soft and transparent, then add everything else and heat through.

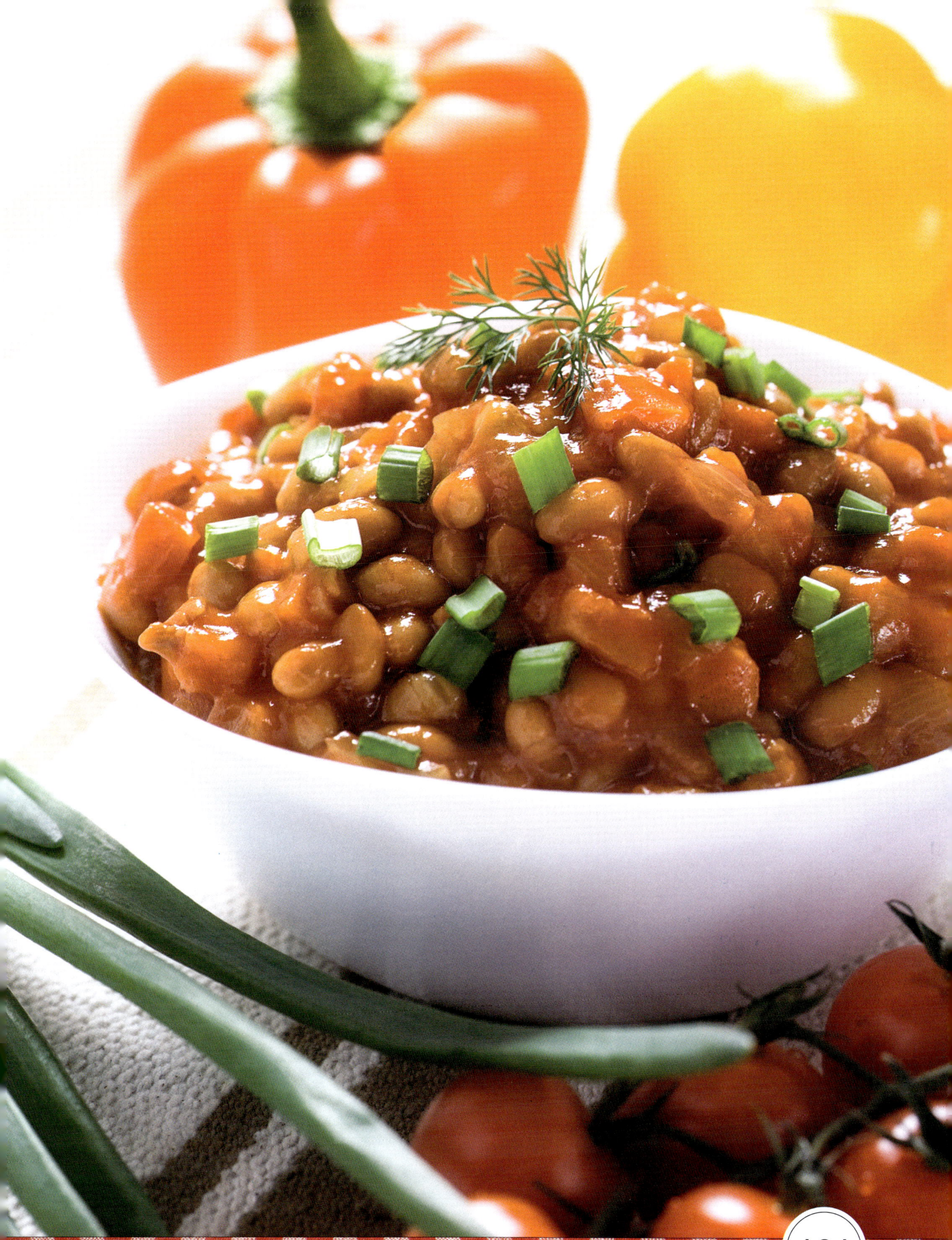

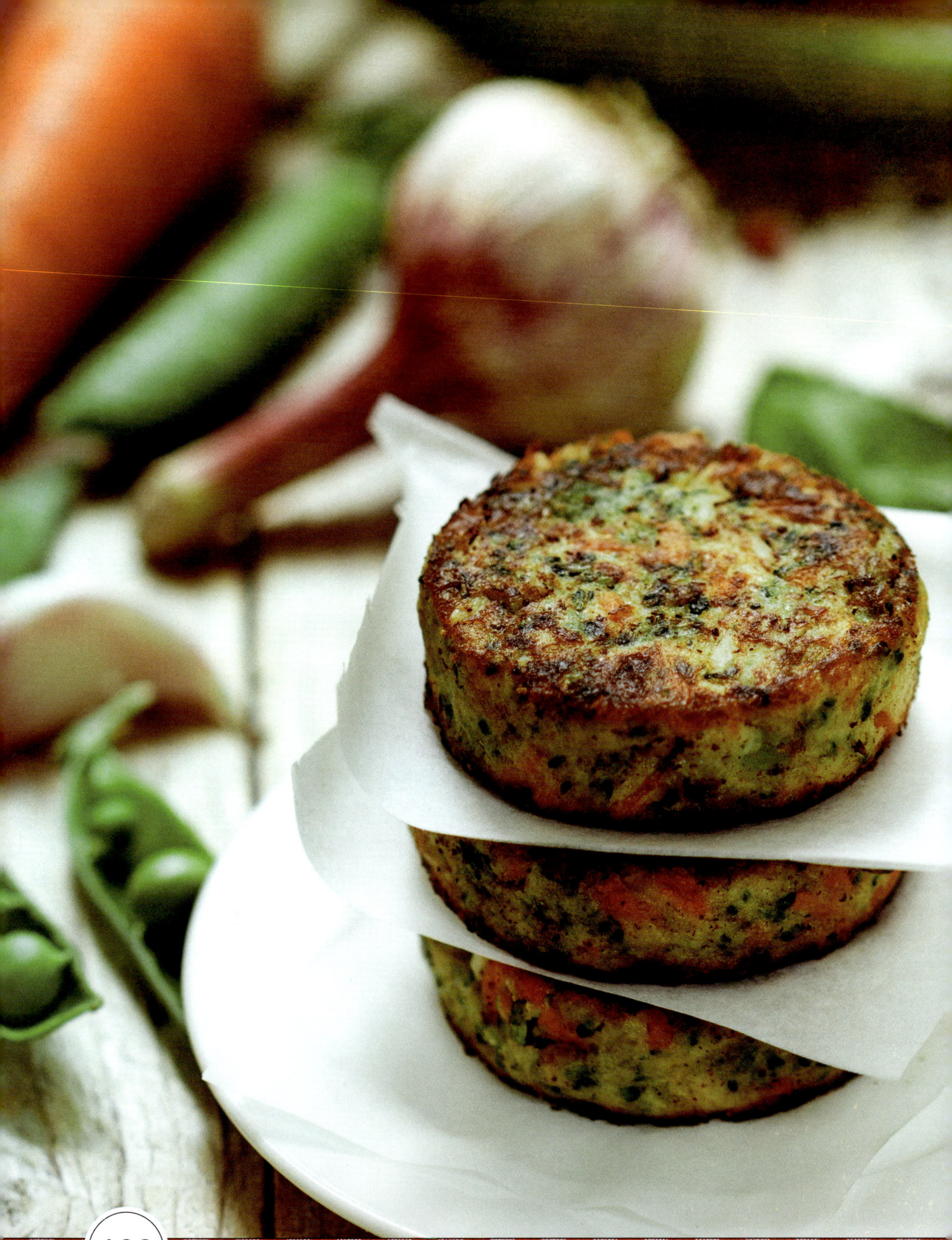

Home-made baked beans
Mix together 1 measure tomato sauce and two measures cooked haricot beans. Bake in a moderately hot oven for 45 to 60 minutes, or until desired consistency is achieved.

Bean and vegetable stew
Start with sautéing onions and celery in a little olive oil or water. For a winter stew, add sliced carrots, chunks of potato, swede, parsnip, your choice of herbs or other flavourings and the ready-cooked beans, plus enough water to keep it from burning. Cook gently until the vegetables are done. For a Provençal flavour use courgettes, peppers, aubergines, tomatoes, ready-cooked beans and flavouring.

Butter bean casserole
1 tin butter beans
1 cupful creamy cashew sauce

Pour the sauce over the beans in a small ovenproof dish and bake in a moderate oven until the top begins to brown.

Bean burgers
Do it all in a food processor if you have one; otherwise, mash beans and chop onion finely.

1 cup beans
1 medium onion
1 cup mashed potato (or breadcrumbs)

Choice of flavourings:
- Tomato purée, oregano, garlic, chopped olives
- Yeast extract, mixed herbs
- Coriander, cumin and garlic

Mix everything together, adding some soya milk or water if necessary. Form into patties or burgers and place on an oiled baking tray. Bake for about half an hour in a moderate oven until golden brown. Serve them in buns with sliced onion, and ketchup or sliced tomato, or for dinner with cooked vegetables and gravy or tomato sauce.

SOYA BEANS, TOFU AND TVP

No discussion about beans is complete without mentioning soya beans and tofu. Soya beans have many remarkable properties, including plant hormone phytochemicals which are thought to help protect against a variety of degenerative diseases. The use of dairy produce is associated with a higher incidence of those problems so it is worth substituting soya products for dairy products.

Cooking the unprocessed soya beans with their full complement of soya goodness takes a long time, even with a pressure cooker.

Tofu cottage cheese

1 250g pack tofu, mashed
1 tsp garlic purée
1 tsp tarragon or other dried herbs
Salt or herb salt to taste
Lemon juice to taste
Soya milk, cream or mayonnaise

Mix together, adding enough nut or soya milk, cream or mayonnaise to make it hold together.

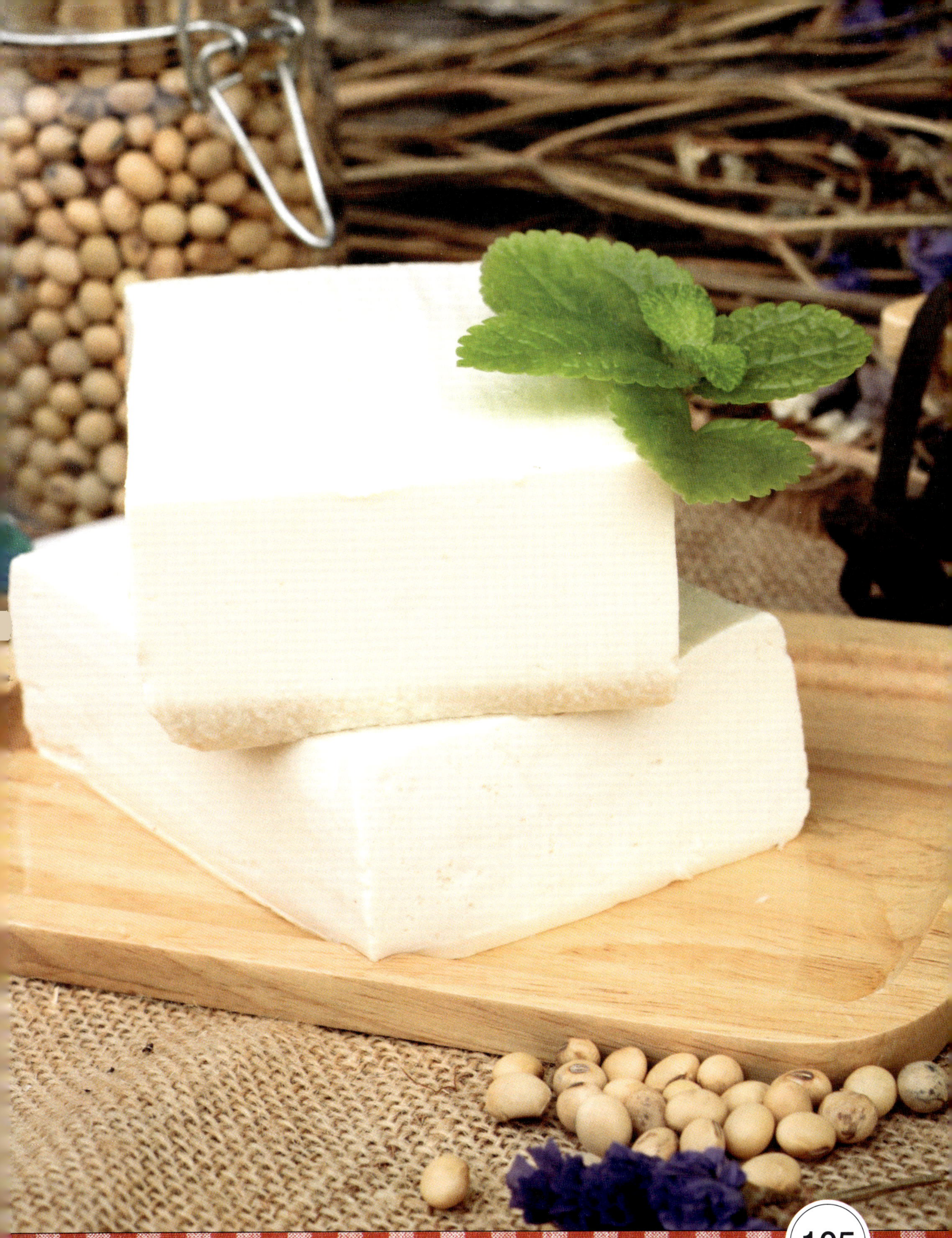

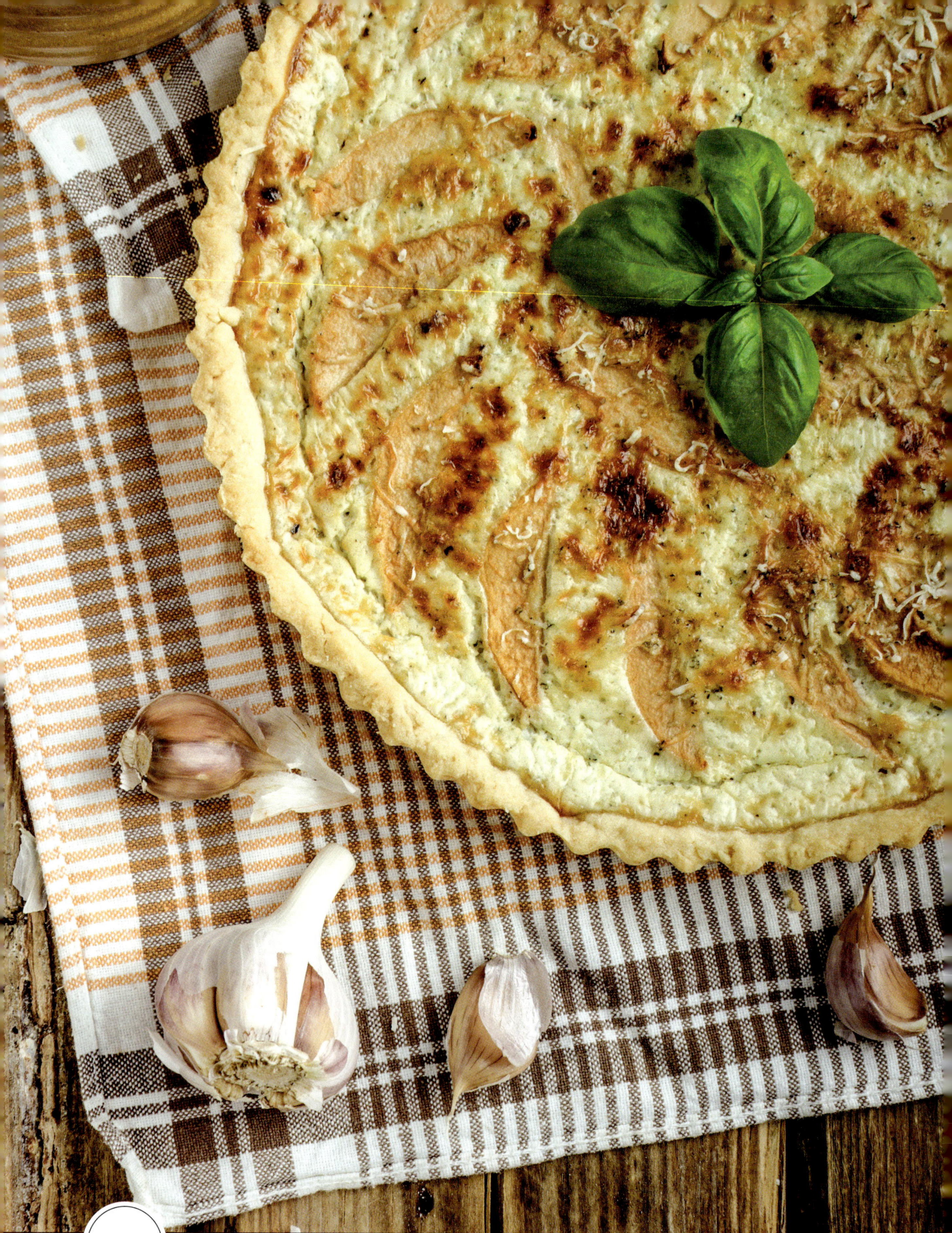

Tofu quiche

1 pack tofu (250g)
1 cup soya milk
2 Tbs flour
Seasoning to taste: herb salt, garlic, yeast flakes
2 cups cooked vegetables

Spread the cooked vegetables in an uncooked pie shell – see the recipe for this on page 124. Whizz the rest of the ingredients in the blender for a few seconds, then pour the mixture over the vegetables in the pie shell. Cook in a moderate oven until the filling becomes solid and the top begins to brown.

Tofu is a processed form of soya, much quicker and easier to deal with. It has lost some of its nutritional elements, but what it lacks in nutrition it makes up for in convenience and prevention of stress. Tofu has very little taste, which makes it very versatile, and it can be used in many different savoury and sweet recipes.

TVP (textured vegetable protein) is made from soya. It is quick and easy to use, and can be very useful when making the transition from a mixed to a vegetarian diet.

Soya in any form, particularly in tofu and TVP, is a concentrated protein, so use it in small quantities. Soya is very widely used in many kinds of processed food, so it is possible to get too much, and some people develop a sensitivity to it. To avoid this, use small quantities, don't use it every day and read labels carefully when you buy pre-made foods.

Tofu lasagne

- For a 9x12-inch pan, spread 1 cup tomato sauce on the bottom.
- Cover with a layer of lasagne noodles.
- Cover this with 1 cup tomato sauce. Crumble 1 cup tofu over the sauce, and dribble 1 cup vegan pimento cheese over the tofu.
- Repeat the lasagne, tomato sauce, tofu and 'cheese' layers once or twice more.
- You can use TVP mince instead of tofu.
- As an optional rich topping use soya mayonnaise as the final layer.
- For a gratin topping, sprinkle fine brown breadcrumbs mixed with yeast flakes and oregano on the top.
- Bake for 45-50 minutes at 200°C. If the top browns too fast, cover with foil.

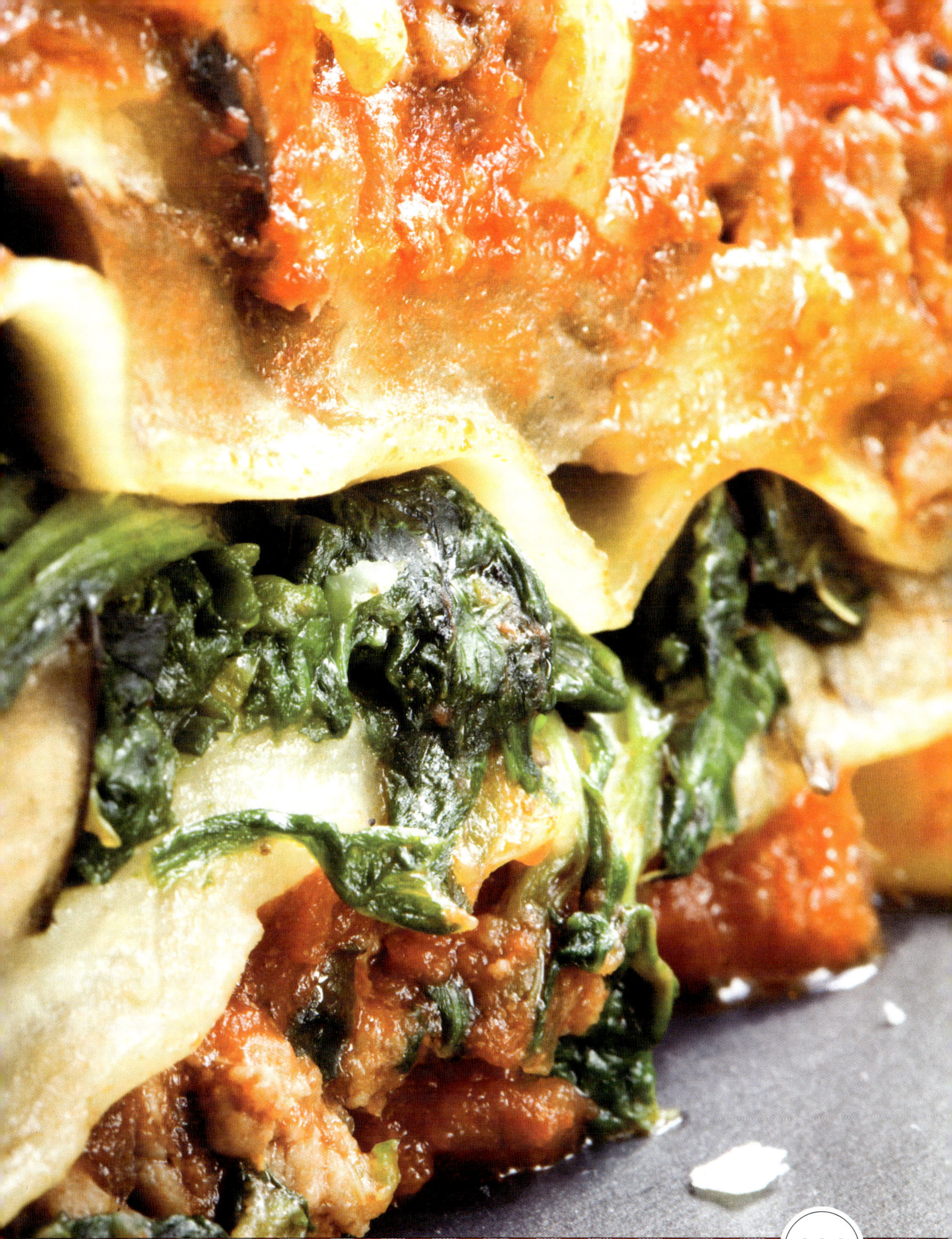

NUTS

Menu planning: nut roast is for eating as part of a main course, with plenty of salad, cooked vegetables, and unrefined starch in the form of potatoes, rice, etc. It is not supposed to be eaten by the plateful on its own. Nut pâté on bread makes a good meal with vegetable soup and salad – avoid high-protein soups like bean or lentil and choose a light raw salad.

Basic savoury nut recipe
(serves four)

1 cup nuts
2 cups breadcrumbs
1 large onion
1 stick celery
½ cup water
1 Tbs yeast extract
1 Tbs mixed herbs

- Make the breadcrumbs and then grind the nuts in the blender.
- Next, blend the onion, celery, yeast extract and ½ cup of water together.
- Now mix everything together and stir in the herbs. The mixture should be moist but firm. Add more water if it is too dry.

For a **nut roast**, put the above mixture in a well-greased loaf tin and cook in a moderate oven for an hour or more, until it is fairly firm. Or put it in a shallow tin or casserole dish, and it will bake more quickly.

For **burgers or patties**, form into balls, then place on an oiled tray, flatten into desired shape and bake in a moderate oven. These will cook much quicker than a roast – in half an hour or less. Turn them once during cooking for a flatter shape.

For **pâté**, bake in the oven until just firm. Cool and spread on bread.

For a **pie**, make a wholewheat oat pie shell, put in a layer of steamed or sautéed onion, then cover with nut roast mixture and bake.

For **stuffed marrow**, first cut the marrow in half lengthwise, scoop out the seeds, and half-cook it in the oven, a steamer or a microwave oven. Then fill the marrow with the nut mixture, and bake in a moderate oven until the marrow is fully cooked and the stuffing is firm and starting to brown.

Variations in ingredients
Choice of nuts: vary your nut roasts by choosing different varieties of nuts, different herbs, different vegetables and even different kinds

of bread or other starches. Peanuts are the cheapest nuts and mix well with most other nuts when used half-and-half. You can also use sunflower seeds to replace half or all of the nuts. For a start, try walnuts with peanuts, or hazelnuts with sunflower seeds.

Choice of vegetables: add a carrot instead of or as well as the onion or celery.

Choice of herbs and other flavourings: the possibilities are endless.

Choice of starchy basis: instead of breadcrumbs you can use mashed potato, cooked rice or cooked millet, reducing the water for blending the onion by at least half a cup. Replacing some of the breadcrumbs, say a quarter to a third, with rye bread adds a rich flavour. The mixture should be moist but firm. If it is too moist, add a handful of porridge oats to absorb the excess moisture.

This is quite a rich nut roast. If you feel it is too rich, simply alter the proportions, reducing the amount of nuts, and/or increasing the amount of the other starch. It's the sort of recipe that really can't easily go wrong.

Simply nutty ideas for enriching and brightening up simple lunches:

To turn plain cooked vegetables into a satisfying main dish, sprinkle liberally with chopped or ground nuts. Try ground walnuts with a little olive oil and garlic for a jacket potato topping or sprinkle a generous spoonful of toasted chopped mixed nuts and seeds over a raw mixed salad.

Nutty rice savoury

2 cups grated carrots
1 cup cooked brown rice
1 medium onion, finely chopped (or ground in blender with tomato juice)
1 cup nuts, chopped, or ground in blender
1 cup brown breadcrumbs
1 cup tomato juice (or tinned tomato)
1 cup chopped olives
1 tsp sage
Salt if the olives don't make it salty enough.

- **Mix everything together** and **bake** in a casserole dish for an hour in a moderate oven.

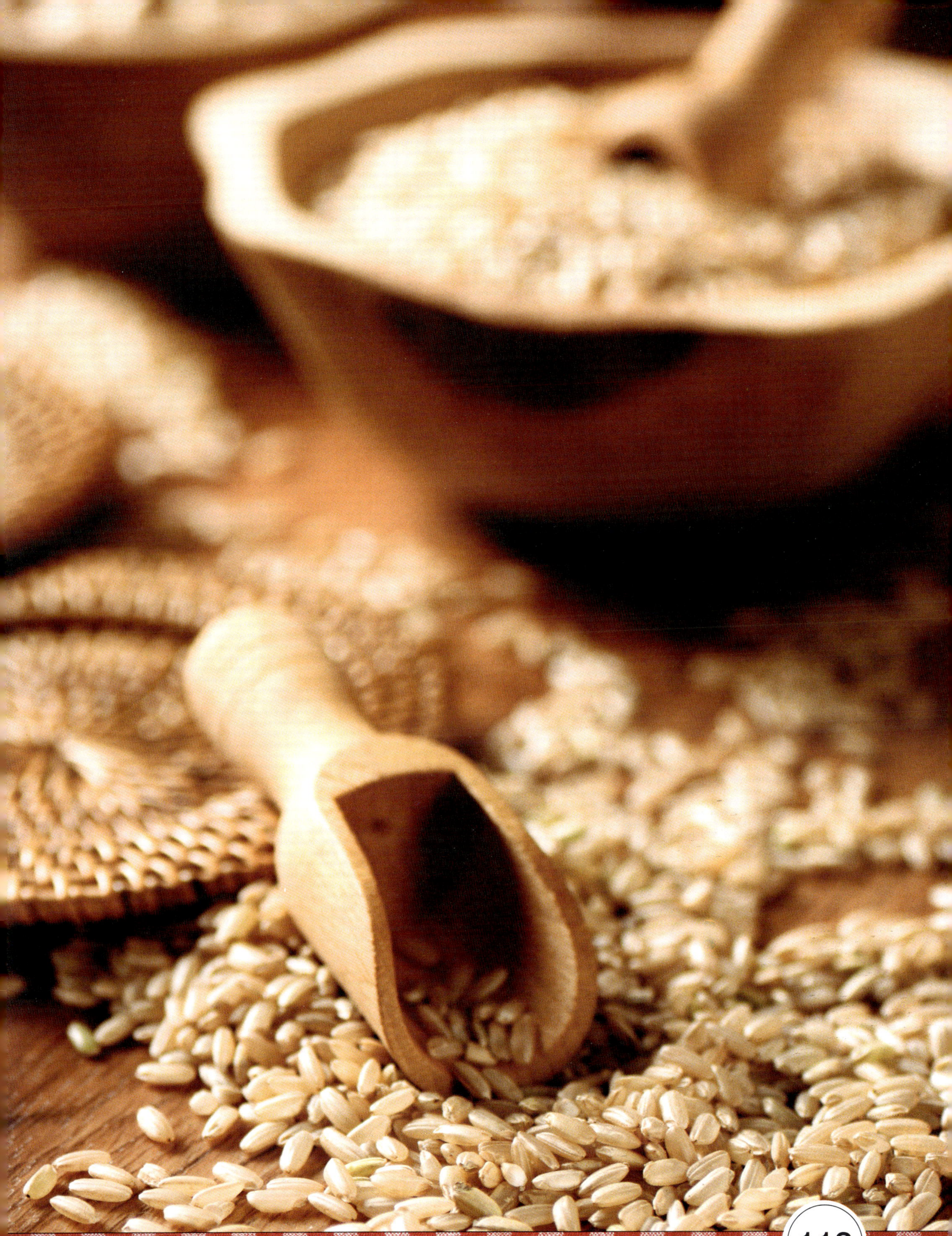

114

Red lentil and cashew nut roast

250g red lentils, washed
150g vegetarian apple-and-herb stuffing mix
100g cashew nuts
1 Tbs tahini (sesame seed paste)
3 cloves garlic
1 tsp cumin
6 Tbs yeast flakes
Juice from ½ lemon
1½ tsp salt
¼ tsp cayenne pepper
5 cups water
2 red peppers, sliced
Bunch of basil or parsley leaves (optional)

- Boil lentils in 4 cups water over medium heat until soft.
- Add the remaining cup of water to the cashew nuts, garlic, cumin, yeast flakes, lemon juice, tahini, salt, cayenne pepper and red peppers in a blender, and blend until fully liquidised.
- Add the lentils to the blended liquid, and fold in the apple-and-herb stuffing mix until completely mixed in.
- Pour mixture into Pyrex dish and bake at Gas Mark 5 for 30 minutes. Leave to cool for 10 minutes, then garnish with parsley or basil and serve (serves 4-6).

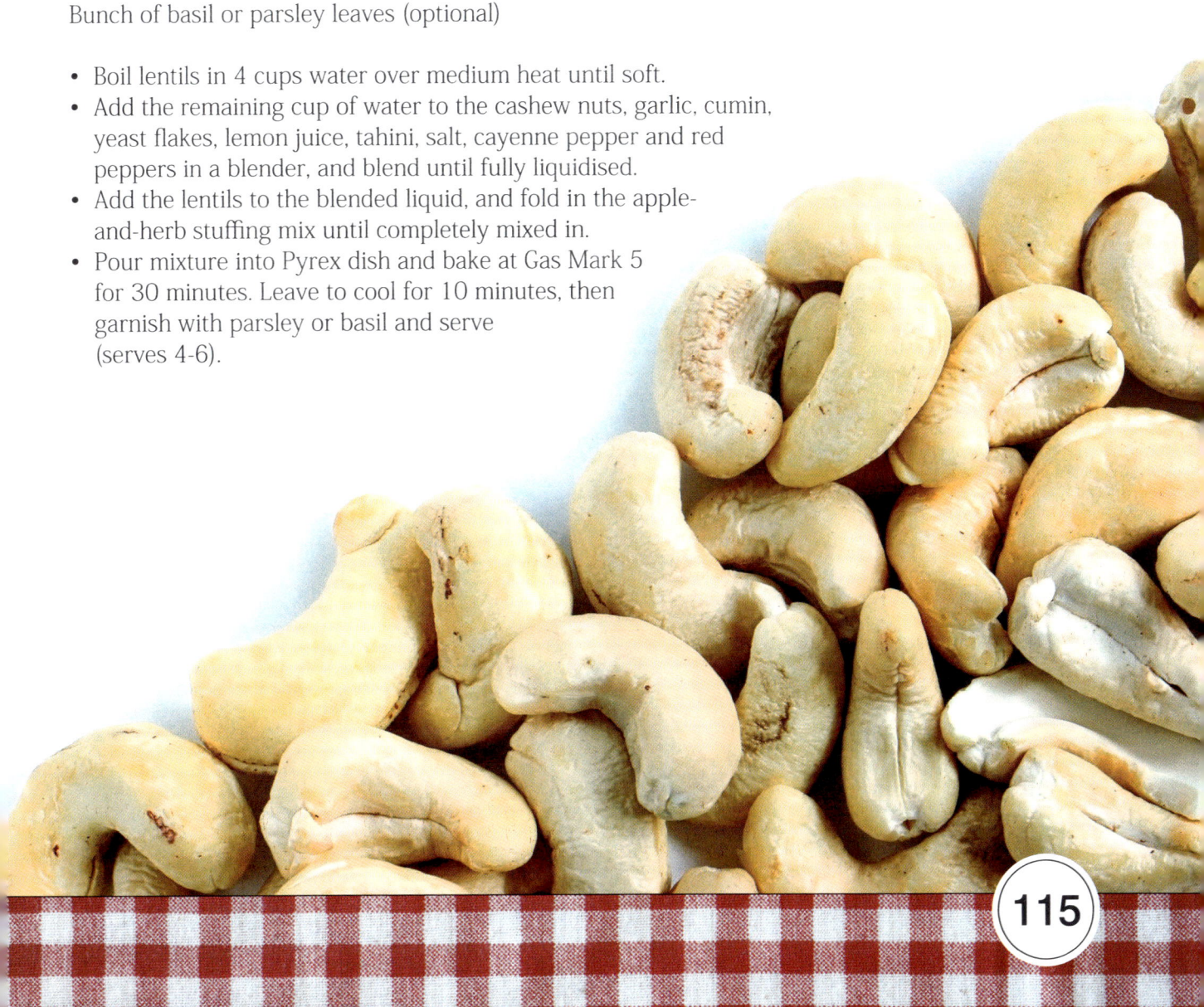

Festive nut roast

This festive nut roast is in three layers, with a lighter-coloured layer in the centre, and prunes and apricots to make it extra special. Enough for 10-12 servings.

Basic dark nut roast mixture for top and bottom layers
2 cups dark-coloured nuts, such as walnuts or walnut/peanut mixture
4 cups wholewheat breadcrumbs
2 medium onions
2 sticks celery
1 cup water
2 Tbs yeast extract (or more, to taste)
2 Tbs mixed herbs

- Make the breadcrumbs and then grind the nuts in the blender.
- Next blend the onion, celery, yeast extract and water together.
- Now mix everything together and stir in the herbs. The mixture should be moist but firm. Add more water if it is too dry.

Middle light nut roast layer
Prepare in the same way, using:
1 cup light-coloured nuts, such as cashews
9-12 ready-to-eat prunes and/or apricots
2 cups lighter-coloured breadcrumbs
1 medium onion
1 stick celery
½ cup water
½ tsp herb salt, or to taste

- Thoroughly grease a loaf tin or deep ovenproof dish.
- Arrange the nut roast mixtures in 3 layers, with the cashew mix in the middle.
- Now take 9-12 ready-to-eat prunes and/or apricots, and stuff them one by one, evenly spaced, into the nut roast.
- Smooth over the top, and bake in a moderate oven for an hour, or until firm and starting to brown.
- Remove from tin or dish and place on a platter, surrounded with roasted cherry tomatoes and button mushrooms. Serve in slices, with relish, gravy and vegetables.

117

118

Nut roast en croûte
(nut roast savoury roll)

This is nut roast mix encased in pastry. This can be wholemeal pastry (see page 124) or, for a special effect, bought flaky pastry, rolled out very thinly. Roll the pastry into a long rectangle.

Make the nut roast mix into a long, thick sausage shape and place it longways in the centre of the pastry rectangle. Bring the two edges of pastry together to enclose the nut roast.

Turn it over, so the join is underneath, and transfer to a baking tray. Brush the top with soya milk, and decorate with diagonal cuts or a criss-cross pattern. Bake in a moderately hot oven until the pastry is golden-brown.

Non-nut savoury roll suggestions:
A savoury festive roll is really just a different shape of pie. Most things that can be put in pies can be used for savoury rolls. You can use any kind of bean, lentil or vegetable stew or roast, but it does need to be fairly dry. You can use porridge oats, rice flakes or breadcrumbs to absorb some of the fluid if it's too moist. Then make it according to the directions for nut roast en croûte.

NUT-FREE ALTERNATIVES

Sunflower and sesame roast
Make as for nut roast, replacing nuts with a mixture of sunflower and sesame seeds. Grind the seeds briefly so a few are still whole.

Lentil roast
This can be turned out as a loaf, or just spooned out of the ovenproof dish.

1 onion, whizzed in blender with 1 stick celery, a medium-sized carrot and 1 cup water
1 cupful red lentils
1 tin chopped tomatoes (2 cups)
½ cupful porridge oats
1 cup water
¼ tsp basil or oregano
1 tsp herb salt or other seasoning to taste
1-2 Tbs olive oil (optional)

Mix everything together, and put it into a rather shallow ovenproof dish. Bake in a moderately hot oven until it is firm – 1-1½ hours.

121

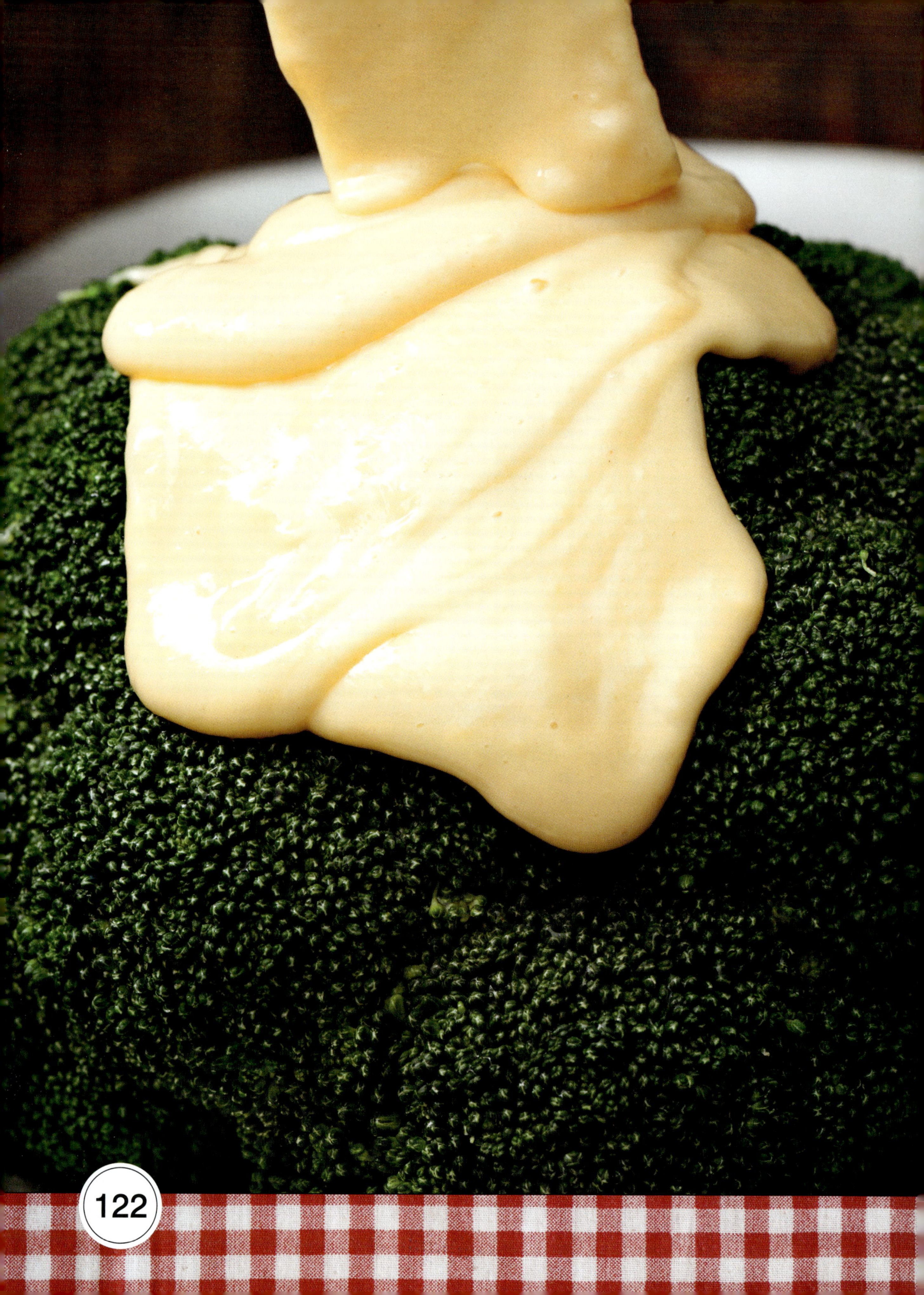

Quick vegan cheese sauce
1 cup cashew pieces cooked for a few minutes in 1 cup water
3 Tbs yeast flakes
1 tsp salt
¼ cup fresh onion
1 clove garlic
½ cup pimento or sweet pepper, cooked or chopped (leave out for white cheese)
2 Tbs lemon juice

Blend until very creamy. Use as it is for pizza, lasagne or 'cheese' on toast. Cook to use as a spread.

Lighter cheese sauce
To make a lighter cheese sauce, for cauliflower cheese, etc: mix one part vegan cheese sauce with one or two parts white sauce (made with 2 Tbs flour to 1 cup soya or other non-dairy milk).

CHEESE
(see also the section on 'cheese' in the 'Breakfasts' chapter)

Do not think of 'cheese substitute', but of 'interesting veggie spreads'. When you get used to them, you may well prefer them, especially as they are lighter and easier to digest than dairy cheese. Use them in sandwiches, on toast or on pizza.

PASTRY

Wholemeal pastry (with oil)
1 cup wholewheat flour
1 cup porridge oats
⅓ cup olive oil
½ cup water

Mix thoroughly and roll out on a sheet of cling film or greaseproof paper. It can be used for quiches, pies or crackers. This makes a crispy pastry, suitable for savoury or sweet pies or tarts. It is very easy to mix, but is inclined to break when rolled out; so, except for very small things, roll out on cling film or greaseproof paper. For a shiny glaze, brush the top of pies with soya milk before cooking.

Depending on how thinly it is rolled out, this recipe should make enough pastry for a 24cm (9½-inch) covered pie, or two slightly smaller open tarts.

100% whole-food no-oil pastry
1 cup porridge oats
1 cup wholewheat flour
1½ cups sunflower seeds (or nuts), finely ground in blender or coffee mill
½-1 cup water

Mix everything together, roll out and use as for wholemeal pastry. For a **pre-cooked pie shell**, roll out pastry and line pie dish, pricking the base with a fork. To ensure that the empty pie shell keeps its shape in the oven, fill it with dried beans (which you can keep for this purpose). Bake it for 15-20 minutes in a moderately hot oven.

Wholemeal pastry crackers
Roll the pastry out **thinly**, cut into a shape of your choice and bake it in a moderately hot oven until golden brown (10-15 minutes).

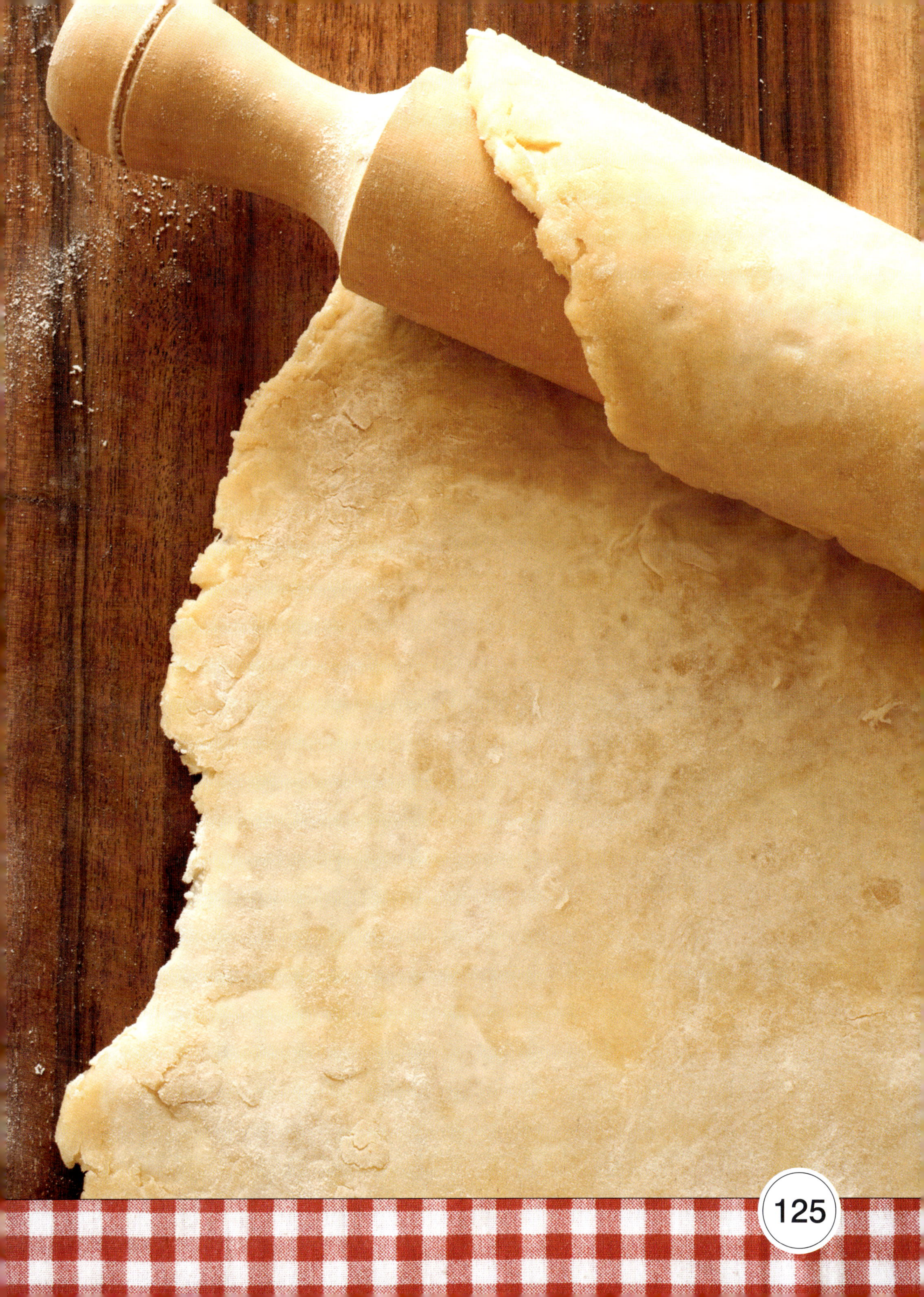

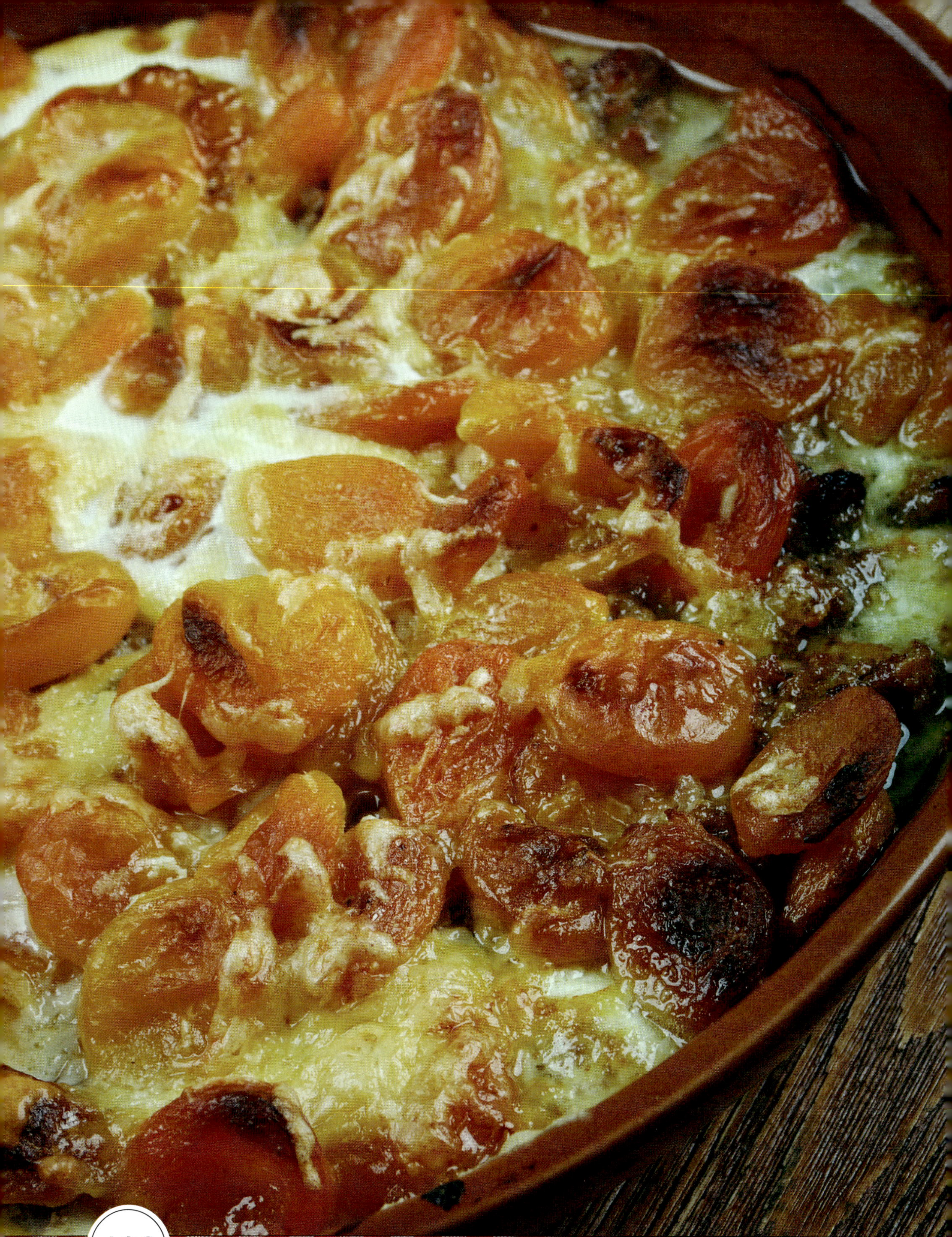

Bobotie

A vegetarian version of a traditional South African dish.

2 cups brown lentils, cooked
1 Tbs mild curry powder
2 medium onions, chopped
1 tsp turmeric
2 cloves garlic, crushed
Pinch of ginger
4 Tbs olive oil
½ cup seedless raisins
2 slices wholewheat bread soaked in water
¼ cup flaked almonds
1 Tbs smooth apricot jam or spread
Salt to taste
1 Tbs lemon juice
1 Tbs fruit chutney*
1½ cups topping sauce**

- Sauté onions and garlic in oil.
- Add all the other ingredients, except for the sauce, and mix gently.
- Place mixture in baking dish and smooth the surface.
- Pour the sauce over the top and bake at 180°C for 45 minutes.
- Serve with yellow rice.

*Quick vinegar-free fruit chutney: mix equal quantities of apricot all-fruit spread or jam and lemon juice.
**Creamy cashew sauce, white sauce, soya or tofu mayonnaise (see pages 36, 92).

Yellow rice to serve with bobotie

2 cups rice
1 tsp salt
1 cinnamon stick
5 cups water
1 tsp turmeric

- Combine ingredients and bring to the boil.
- Lower heat and simmer gently until rice is soft and water is absorbed.
- You can use either brown or white rice for this recipe.

Spinach cakes

½ kilogram spinach, washed
2 spring onions
1 large onion
1 red pepper
1 yellow pepper
1 green pepper
¼ tsp cayenne pepper
½ kilogram wholewheat flour
Pinch of sea salt to taste

- Chop and mix all vegetables, then pour hot water over them to soften them.
- Add flour, and salt (if required), and mix well in a bowl to a soft consistency, forming the mixture into bite-size cakes.
- Sauté the cakes until crispy on the outside.

129

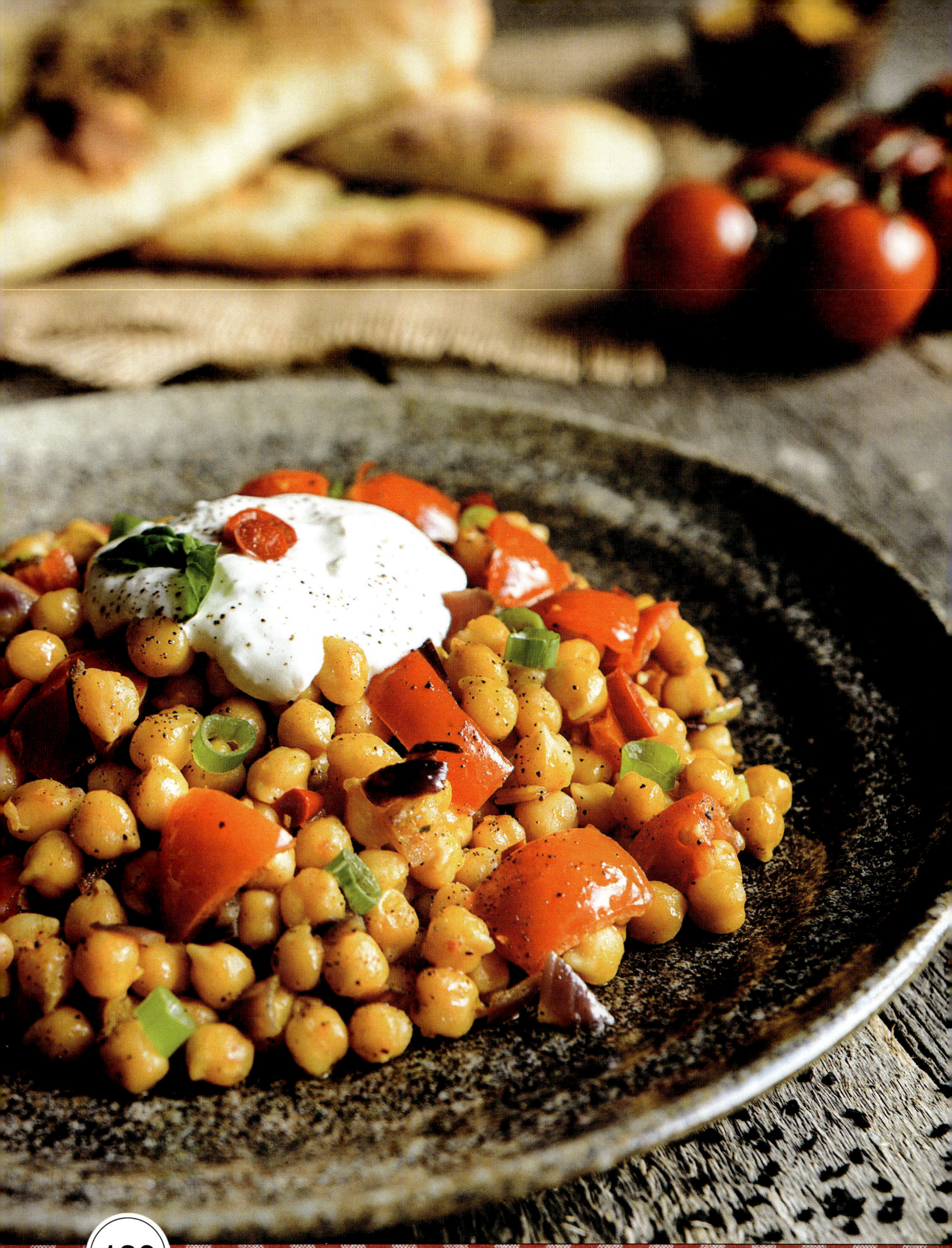

Curry channa/chickpeas

1 tin chickpeas
2 tsp curry powder
1 small onion, sliced
3 cloves garlic, chopped
1 tsp oil
1 pinch salt

- Pre-heat oil in saucepan, then sauté onion and garlic together.
- Add curry powder; then drain chickpeas and add to the pan.
- Cook gently for a further 5-10 minutes, and add a little water and salt to taste.

Carrot and spinach pie

2 large carrots, washed and peeled
½ kilogram spinach, washed
2 large garlic cloves, whole
¼ tsp cayenne pepper
1 Tbs olive oil
1 Tbs sesame seeds
1 pinch celery salt

- Steam carrot, and then slice lengthways.
- Steam spinach with whole garlic cloves, cayenne pepper, celery salt and oil.
- Mix carrot pieces with spinach and place in a Pyrex dish, garnishing with sesame seeds.
- Place under grill until seeds are dark brown. Serve with rice or potatoes.
- This dish is excellent as it stands; however, if you wish to encase it in a pastry shell, see page 124.

133

HAYSTACKS

This is a favourite Mexican-inspired meal. It has a variety of tastes and textures, and it's very easy to make. It consists of a red bean stew, served on tortilla chips, with a variety of salads which can be piled on the top of the beans – like a haystack.

Red bean stew
1 small chopped onion
1 Tbs olive oil with 1 Tbs water
1 small chopped sweet pepper, red or green
1 tin red beans, drained
1-2 crushed garlic cloves
1 tin chopped tomatoes

- Gently sauté the onion, pepper and garlic in the oil and water.
- Add the beans and tomatoes; seasonings such as cumin, sweet paprika and whatever other herbs or spices you like; and salt to taste.
- Add some veggie meat or mince if you want to.
- Let it simmer while you assemble the other things. It should be quite thick.

Vegan sour cream (oil-free sunflower or cashew cream dressing)
½ cup sunflower seeds or cashew nuts, or a mixture
2 Tbs lemon juice
½ tsp herb salt

- Add just enough water to cover the seeds and allow the blender blades to turn easily.
- Blend until smooth, then add lemon juice and salt. For a thinner cream, add extra water at the end.
- Optional: add a clove of fresh garlic, ¼ tsp garlic powder or ½ tsp garlic purée before blending.

Guacamole
1 large ripe avocado
1 Tbs lemon juice (or to taste)
1 small clove garlic, crushed
Salt to taste

- Mash everything together.

Now arrange the rest of the haystack feast:
Tortilla chips – these are the one essential, and in addition serve any or all of the following:
Sliced olives, preferably the pimento stuffed kind

Tomatoes, chopped
Cucumber, sliced or diced
Onions, thinly sliced or chopped
Lettuce, shredded
Mashed avocado or guacamole
Cashew pimento 'cheese' sauce (see pages 46, 47)
Vegan sour cream or soya mayonnaise (pages 92, 93)

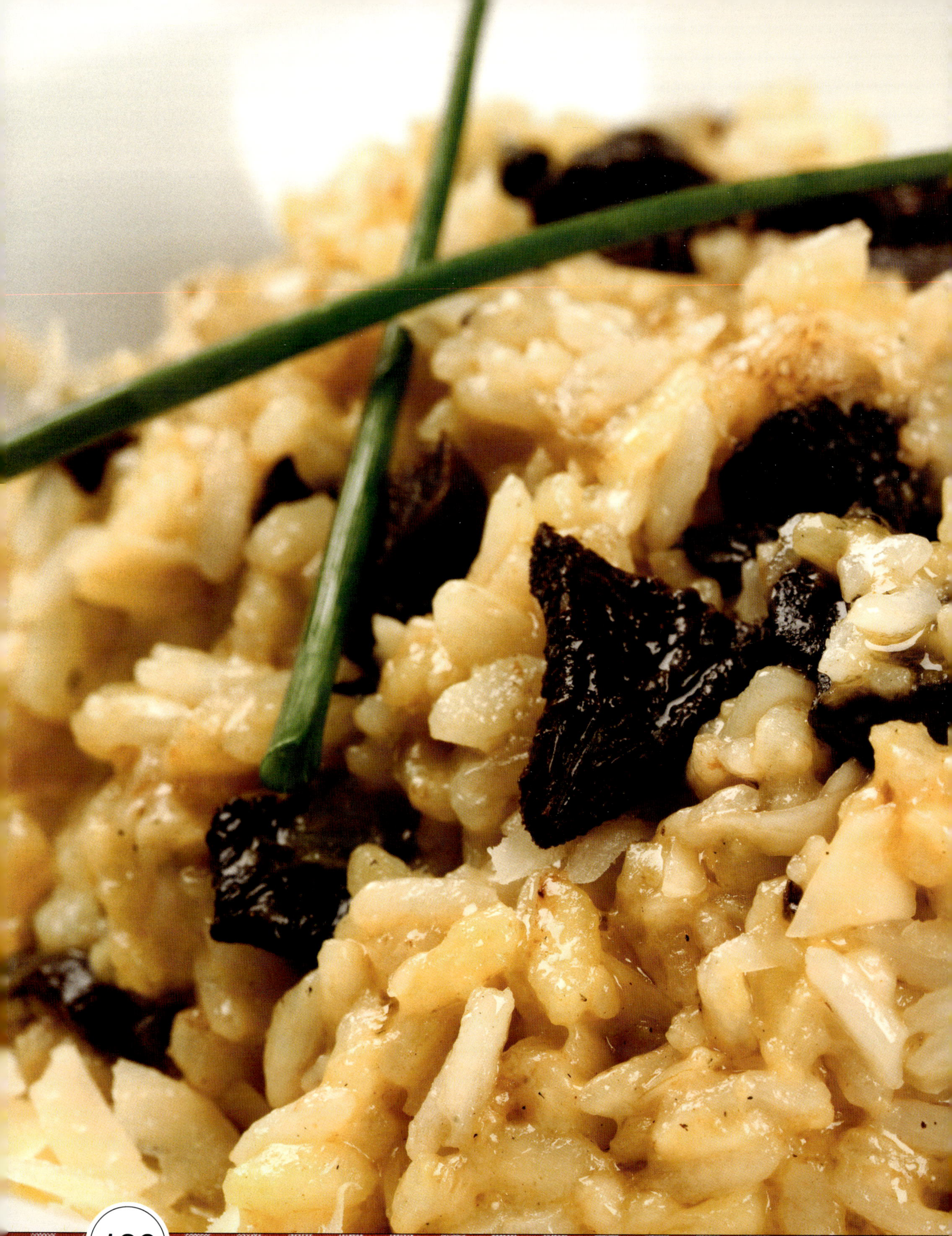

Jollof rice

1 kilogram rice
½ kilogram mixed vegetables and peas
2 large onions
1 tin chopped tomatoes
1½ tsp oil
2 Tbs tomato purée
½ tsp each of mixed herbs, ginger, garlic, cumin
¼ tsp each of cloves, thyme, cayenne pepper
3 vegetable stock cubes or bouillon
½-1 cup water (may vary)
1 cup cabbage, finely chopped (optional)

- Sauté onions and garlic in oil, and then add ginger, tomatoes, tomato purée, cumin, mixed herbs and cayenne pepper. Cook for 4-5 minutes or until sauce reduces. Add stock cubes and salt to taste.
- Rinse the rice and add to sauce, boiling for 2 minutes.
- Reduce heat, stirring occasionally, and add mixed vegetables and water (as needed).
- Continue to fluff rice until fluid is absorbed and rice is cooked.
- Spread cabbage on top in final 5-10 minutes of cooking. Serves 8.

Coconut saffron rice

2 cups basmati or Thai jasmine rice
2 cups good-quality coconut milk
1¾ cups vegetable stock
2½ Tbs dry shredded coconut (unsweetened)
1 tsp turmeric
¼-½ tsp saffron threads
1 clove garlic, minced
1 Tbs soy sauce
1 Tbs lemon juice
1 Tbs cumin
¼ tsp cayenne pepper
2 green onions, chopped

- Place stock in a pot and set over a high heat, and then add turmeric, saffron, garlic, soy sauce, lemon juice, cumin and cayenne pepper. Stir well and bring to boil.
- Rinse and add the rice, and also add shredded coconut and coconut milk. Stir continuously while bringing liquid back to gentle boil.
- Reduce to low heat, cover pot and cook for a further 15 minutes, or until liquid has been reduced.
- Turn off heat and leave covered for another 5-10 minutes; then fluff rice with fork and taste for salt before garnishing with green onions. If too salty, add a squeeze of lemon juice. Enjoy!

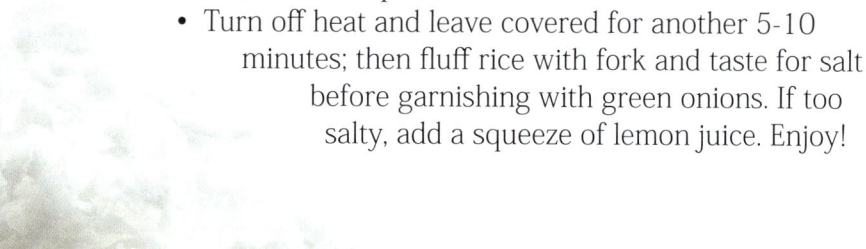

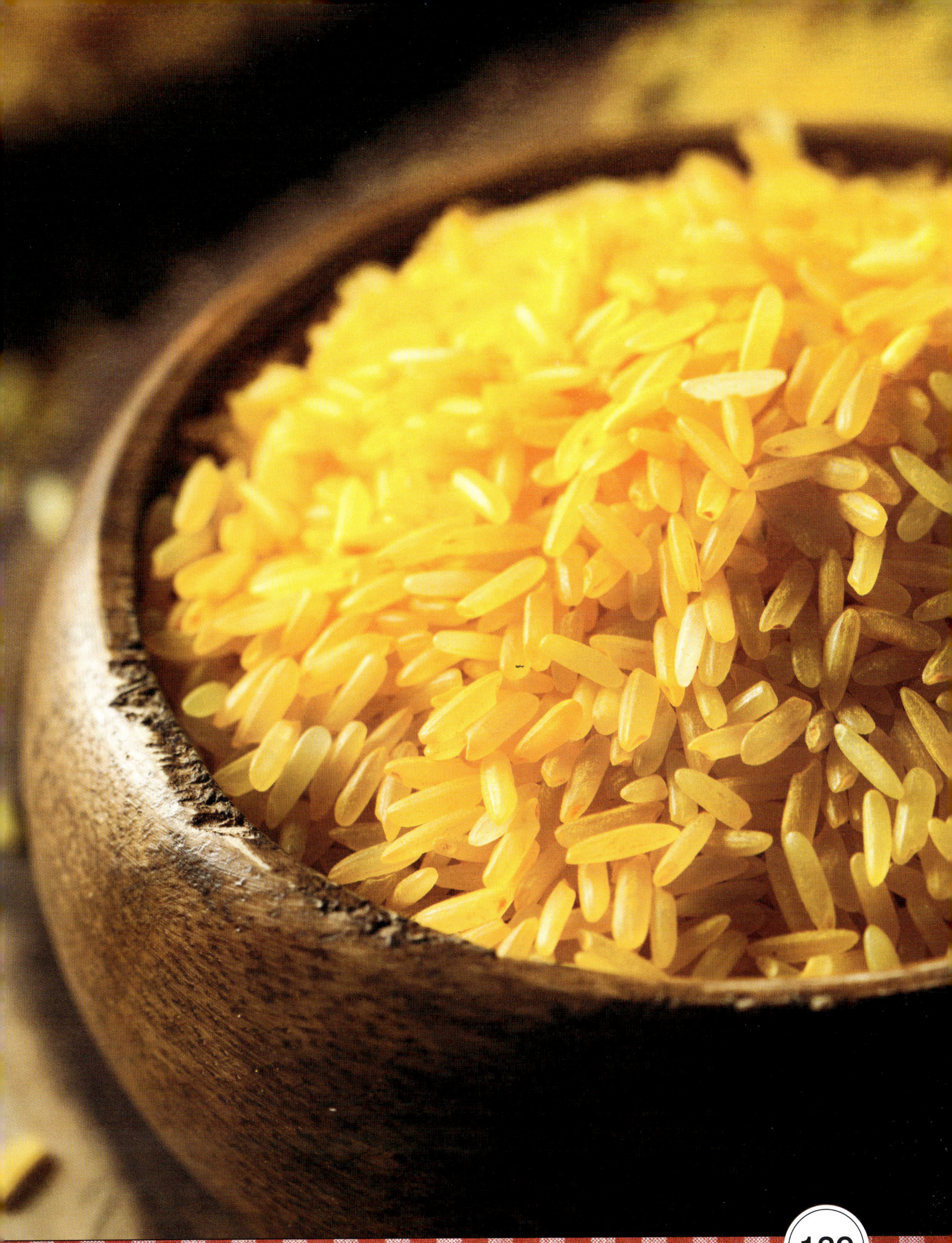

140

Moy moy

500g dry, uncooked black-eyed beans
4 cloves garlic
1 tsp salt
100g tomato paste
1 tsp cayenne pepper
2 Tbs olive oil
1 large onion, chopped

- Put beans in blender or coffee mill and grind until broken in small pieces (not too fine), and then soak overnight in water.
- After soaking, rub beans in hands (wash your hands thoroughly first!) so that the skins come off.
- Blend beans with all other ingredients and either pour into small tins or form balls to place in foil.
- Place in a covered saucepan of boiling water for an hour, or until firm. Serve with a salad.

Nyoyo

½ cup dry maize kernels
½ cup dry red beans
½ cup dry red peanuts (optional)
Water to cook
Salt to taste

- Thoroughly wash maize kernels, beans and peanuts, then soak overnight in water.
- Put mixture in a pot and add water, and then cook until soft (approx. 1½ hours).
- Add salt, if necessary, when almost ready, and stir.
- Allow to simmer for a few minutes, and then serve. Serves 4.

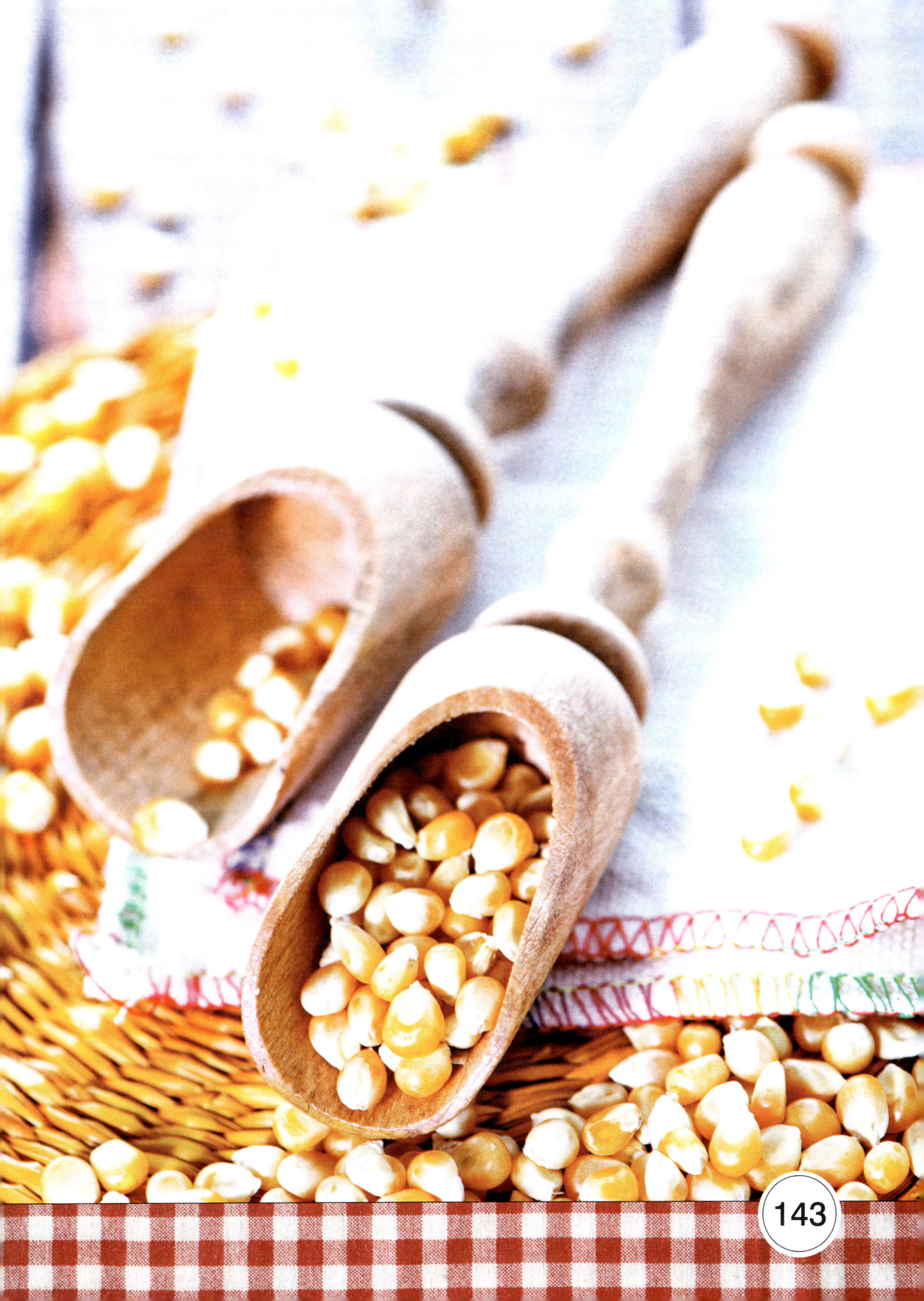

DESSERTS

Introduction

A healthy, balanced diet doesn't have to be boring: so I have included a good selection of tasty, tantalising desserts and some festive food that is relatively easy to make. I hope you enjoy them, remembering not to overindulge of course.

DESSERTS RECIPES
TARTS, PIES AND CHEESECAKES

Wholemeal pastry (with oil)*
(Repeated from page 124 for your convenience)
1 cup wholewheat flour
1 cup porridge oats
⅓ cup olive oil
½ cup water
*To make a sweet pastry, substitute apple juice concentrate or honey for some of the water.

Mix thoroughly and roll out on a sheet of cling film or greaseproof paper. It can be used for quiches, pies or crackers. This makes a crispy pastry, suitable for savoury or sweet pies or tarts. It is very easy to mix, but is inclined to break when rolled out, so, except for very small things, roll out on cling film or greaseproof paper. For a shiny glaze, brush the top of pies with soya milk before cooking.
    Depending on how thinly it is rolled out, this recipe should make enough pastry for a 24cm (9½-in) covered pie, or two slightly smaller open tarts.

100% whole-food no-oil sweet pastry
1 cup porridge oats
1 cup wholewheat flour
1 cup date butter (dates softened or blended in just enough water to cover them)
1½ cups sunflower seeds (or nuts), finely ground
½-1 cup water

Mix everything together, roll out and use as for wholemeal pastry. For a **pre-cooked pie shell**, roll out pastry and line pie dish, pricking the base with a fork. To ensure that the empty pie shell keeps its shape in the oven, fill it with dried beans (which you can keep for this purpose). Bake it for 15-20 minutes in a moderately hot oven.

Crunchy granola base
Easiest crunchy base for a creamy pie or cheesecake: just spread granola in the bottom of the dish (see the recipes for granola in the chapter on 'Breakfasts', pages 32 and 33).
    Standard granola base: briefly grind 2 cups granola or other crunchy cereal, and mix with about 3 Tbs water or orange juice and 1 tsp ground coriander. Press mixture over base of dish. This is suitable for an 8x10-inch (20x25cm) dish. If the pie filling is not to be cooked and you want the base to be crunchy, bake until dry in a moderate oven.

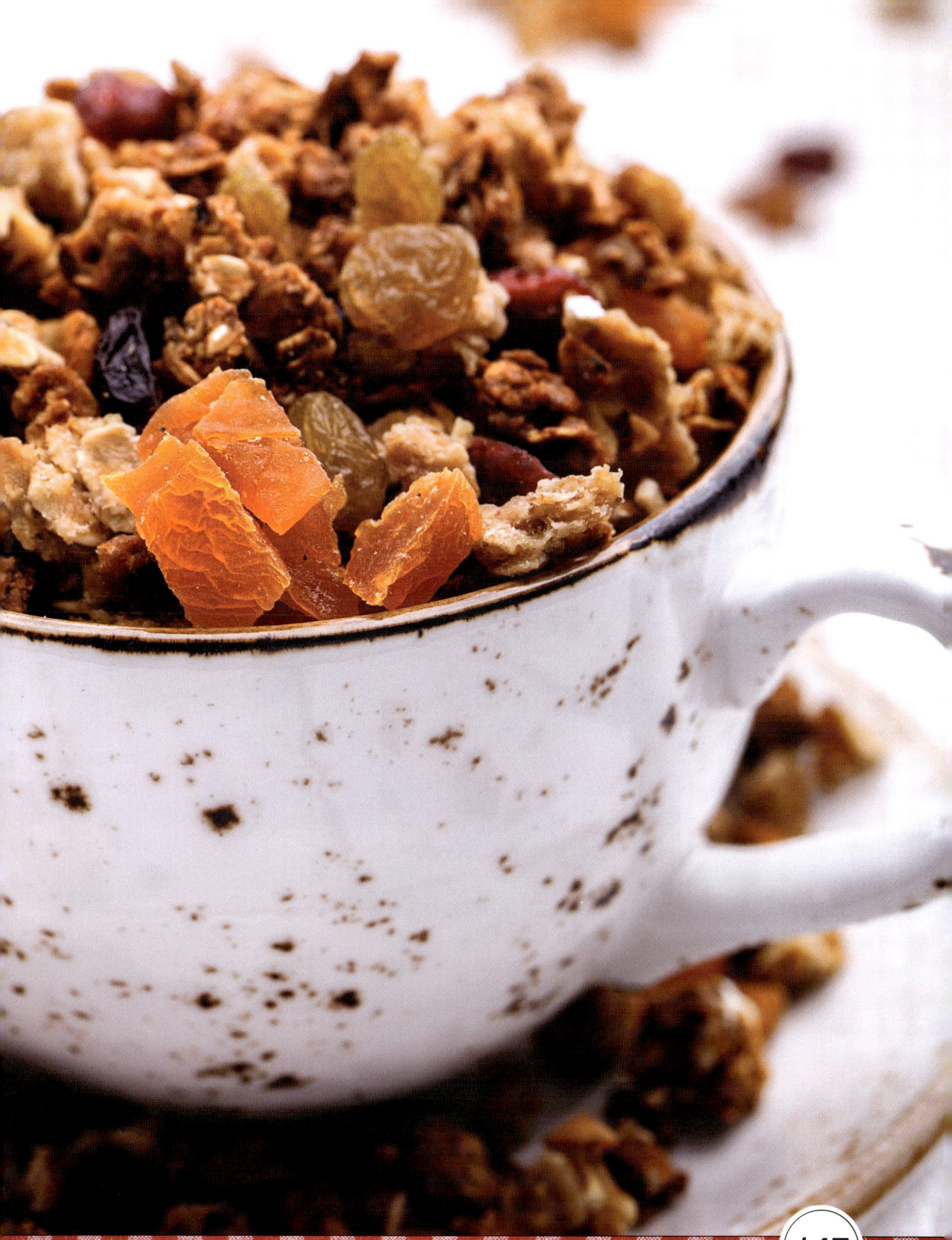

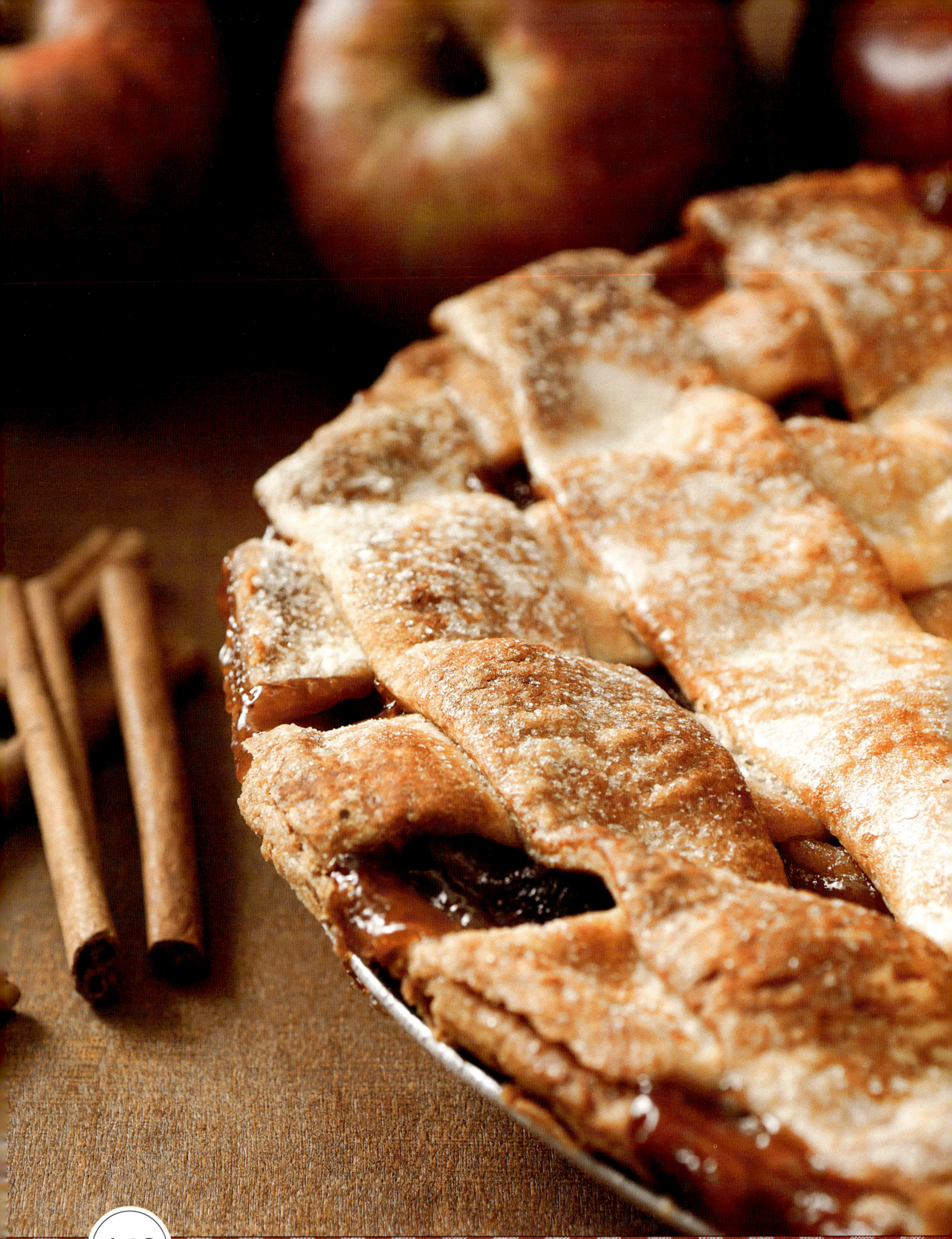

Apple pie

Wholemeal pastry – see page 146. Use a little more than half of the pastry for the base.

Filling:
2-3 cooking apples
½-1 cup raisins

- Peel and slice the apples. Fill the pie shell with alternate layers of raisins and sliced apples. Cover with the rest of the pastry, making a small central hole to let the steam out. Brush the top with soya milk.
- Instead of raisins, you can sweeten with ¼-½ cup apple juice concentrate. Bake in a moderately hot oven until the top is golden brown.

French apple tart

1 uncooked pastry base
Whole-fruit jam or other fruit spread
Apple sauce (whole apples, cut in chunks, cooked, blended and sieved)
2 or 3 cooking apples, cut in slices
Apple juice concentrate

- Spread the pastry base with jam or spread. Add a thin layer of apple sauce and arrange the apple slices on this, overlapping them, in a circular pattern. Lastly, drizzle apple juice concentrate over the top.
- Cook in a moderately hot oven for at least half an hour. Cover with a piece of foil if the apples are browning too fast.

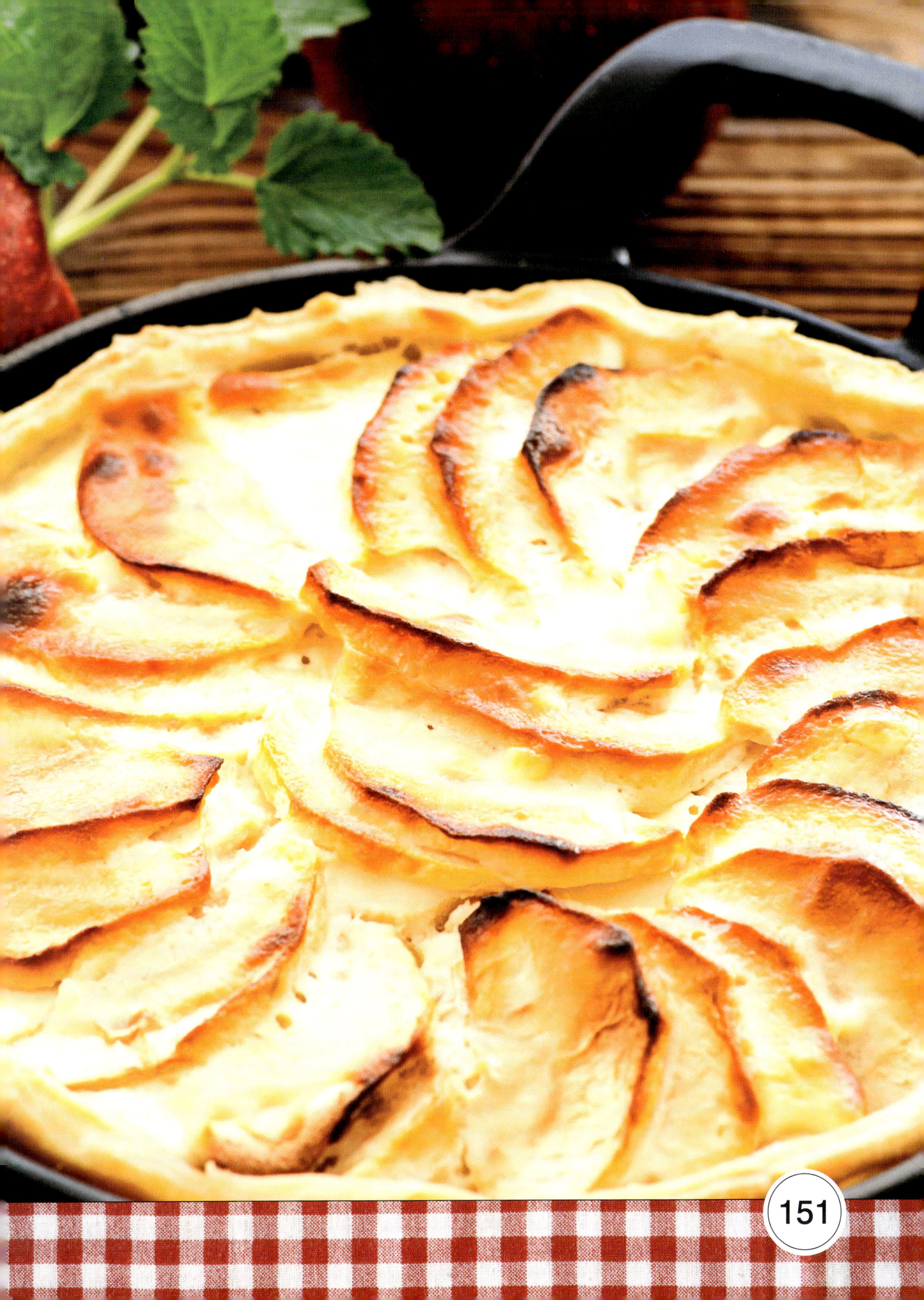

152

Lemon tart

Blend:
3 cups pineapple juice
¼-½ cup honey or apple juice concentrate
½ cup orange juice
2 tsp oil (optional)
¼-⅓ cup lemon juice
Grated rind of 1 lemon
⅓ cup cornflour

Cook over medium heat, stirring until thick, then pour into baked pie shell or onto granola base and cool.

Pineapple cream pie

1 cup cashews
1½ cups pineapple juice
3 Tbs lemon juice
1-2 cups tinned crushed pineapple
¼ cup cornflour

Blend the cashews until smooth in just enough juice to cover them, then blend in everything else except the crushed pineapple. Transfer to a saucepan and cook until it thickens, stirring all the time. Stir in the crushed pineapple and transfer to a baked pie shell.

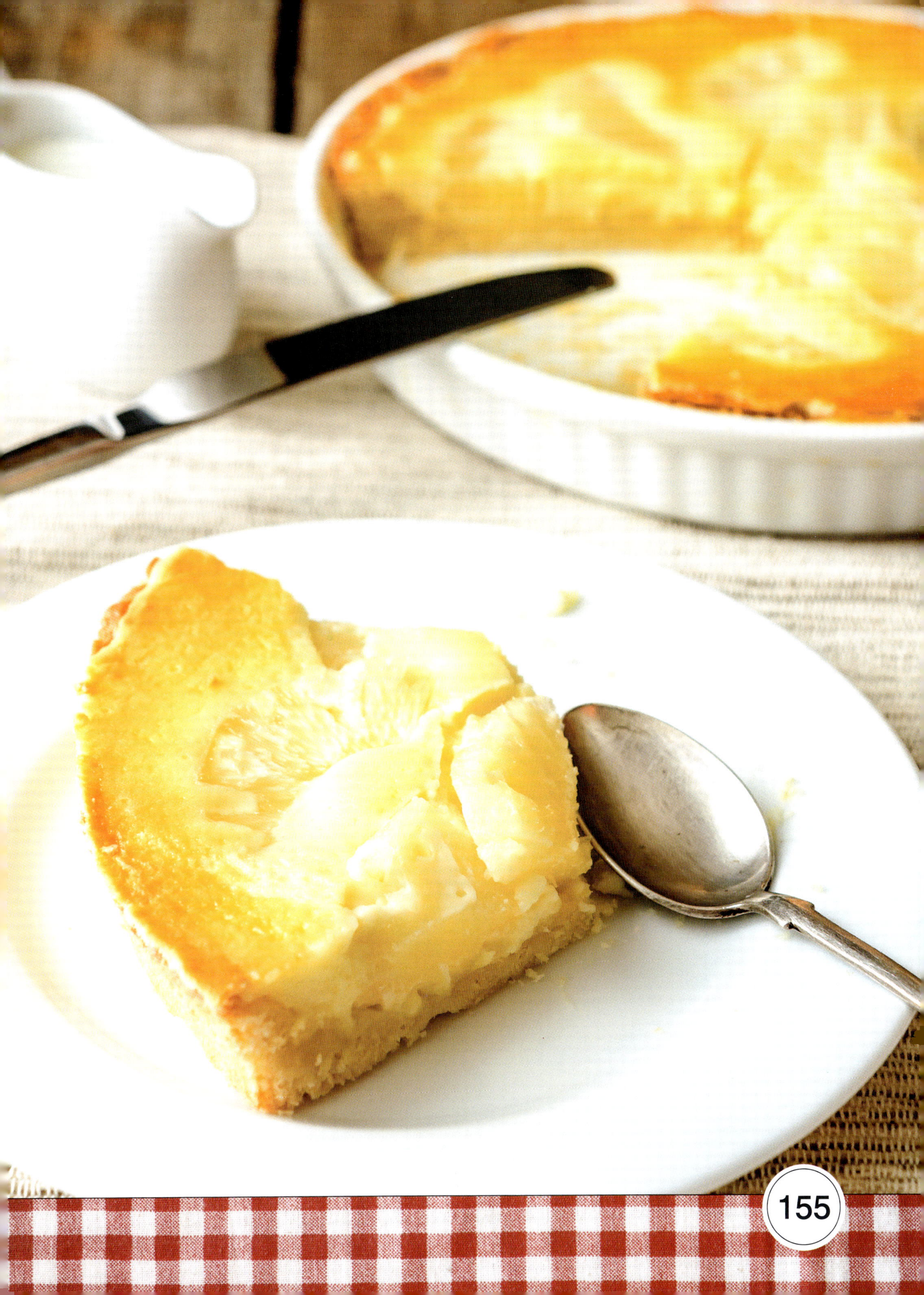

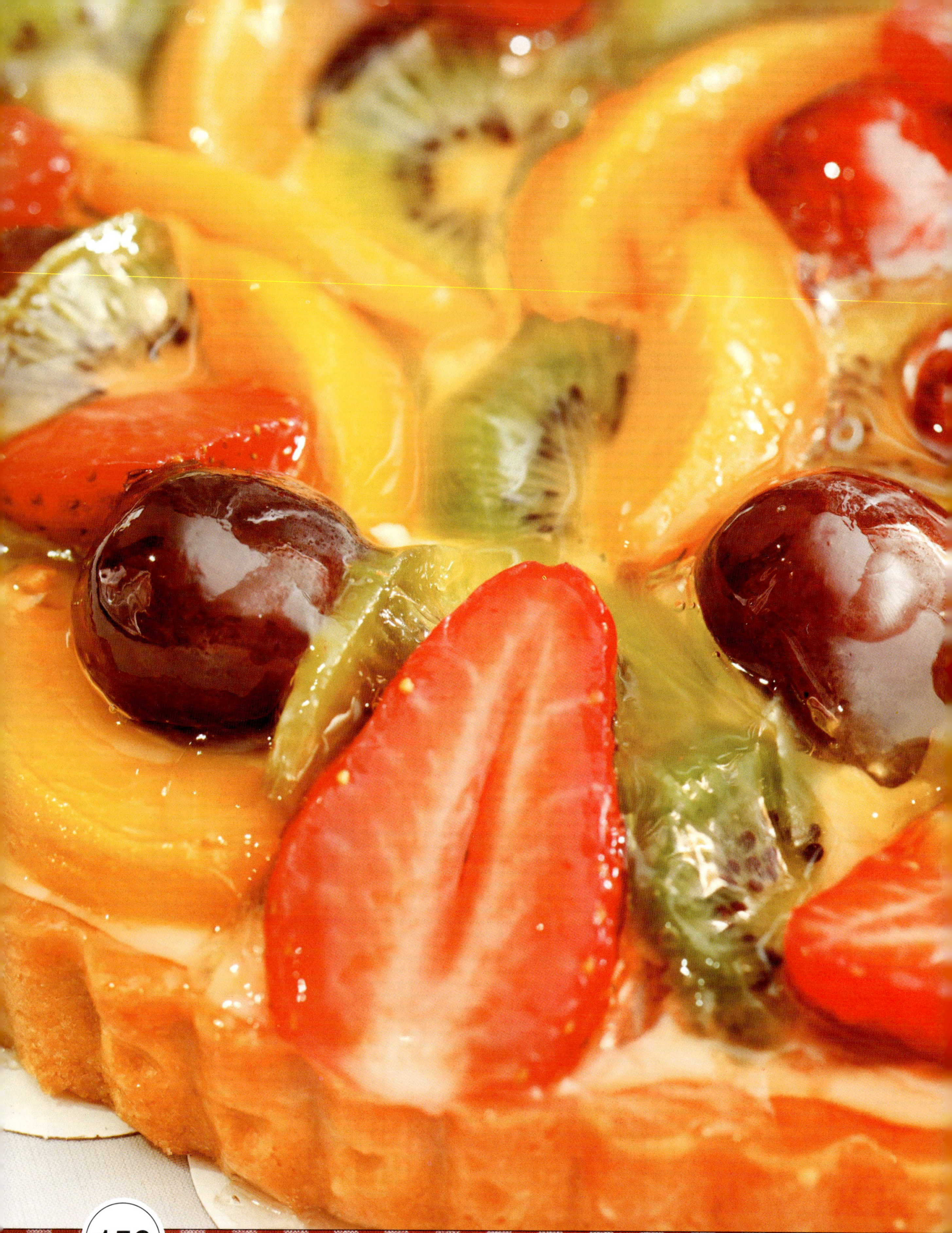

Fruit tart

Spread a baked pie shell with whole-fruit jam or other fruit spread, then cover with apricot halves, sliced peaches, raspberries or other fruit. Pour agar jelly mixture over and serve when cooled.

Agar jelly topping for fruit tarts and cheesecakes
1 cup red grape juice (or other sweet fruit juice)
1¼ Tbs agar flakes

Mix together and bring to the boil, stirring constantly. Allow to cool and thicken a little, then pour over fruit in tart, or spread on top of cheesecake.

Carob pie

2 cups hot water
1 cup raw cashews
1-2 cups dates (depending on how sweet you like it) softened in 1-2 cups hot water
¼-⅓ cup carob powder
¼ cup cornflour
1-2 tsp vanilla

Blend the cashews smooth in just enough of the hot water to cover them. Then add the rest of the water and the other ingredients and blend again. Transfer to a saucepan and cook, stirring constantly, until it thickens, then pour over granola base. Sprinkle with toasted flaked almonds or desiccated coconut.

This is good as a pudding as well – just let it cool in a serving dish instead of a pie shell. It's particularly good served with sliced bananas.

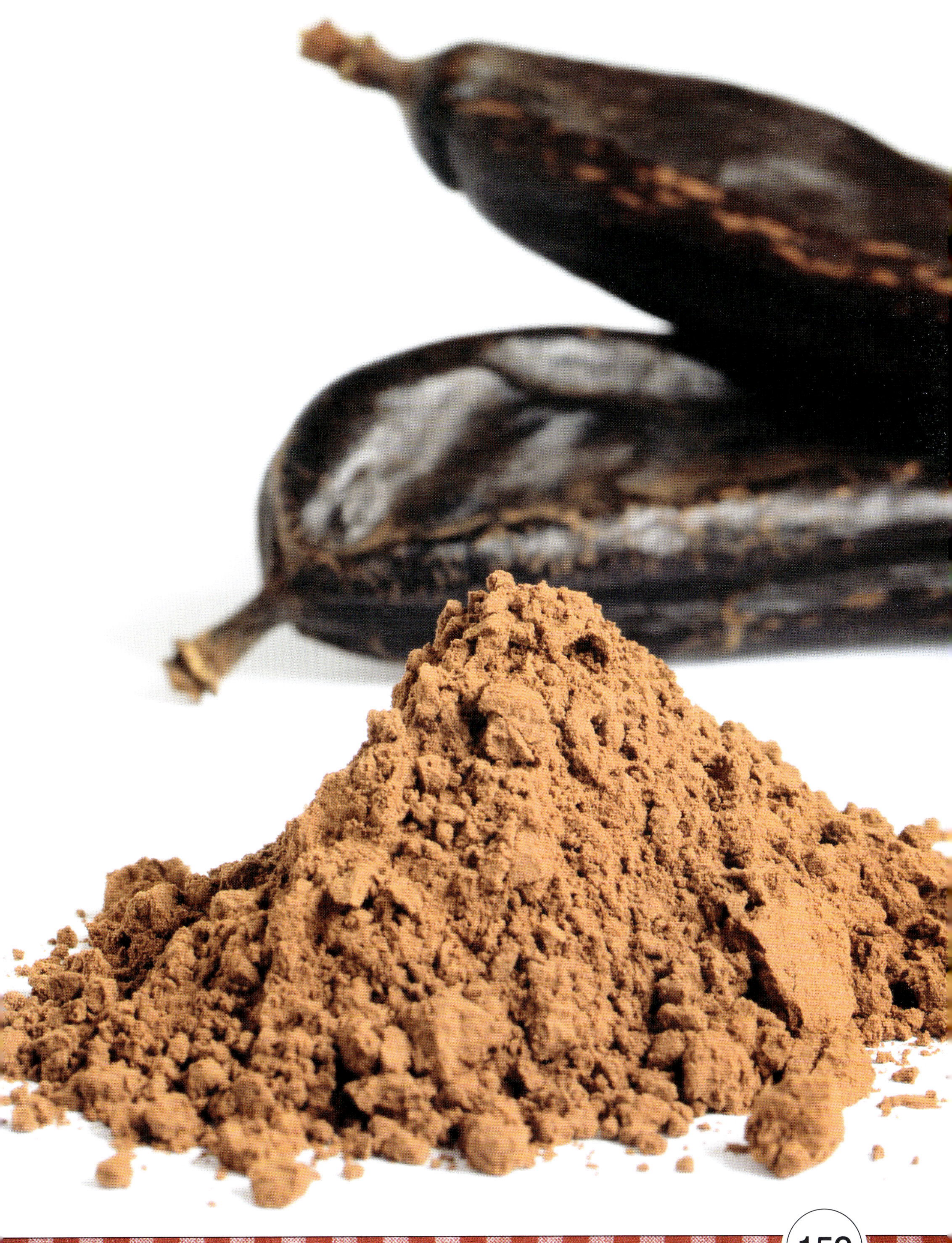

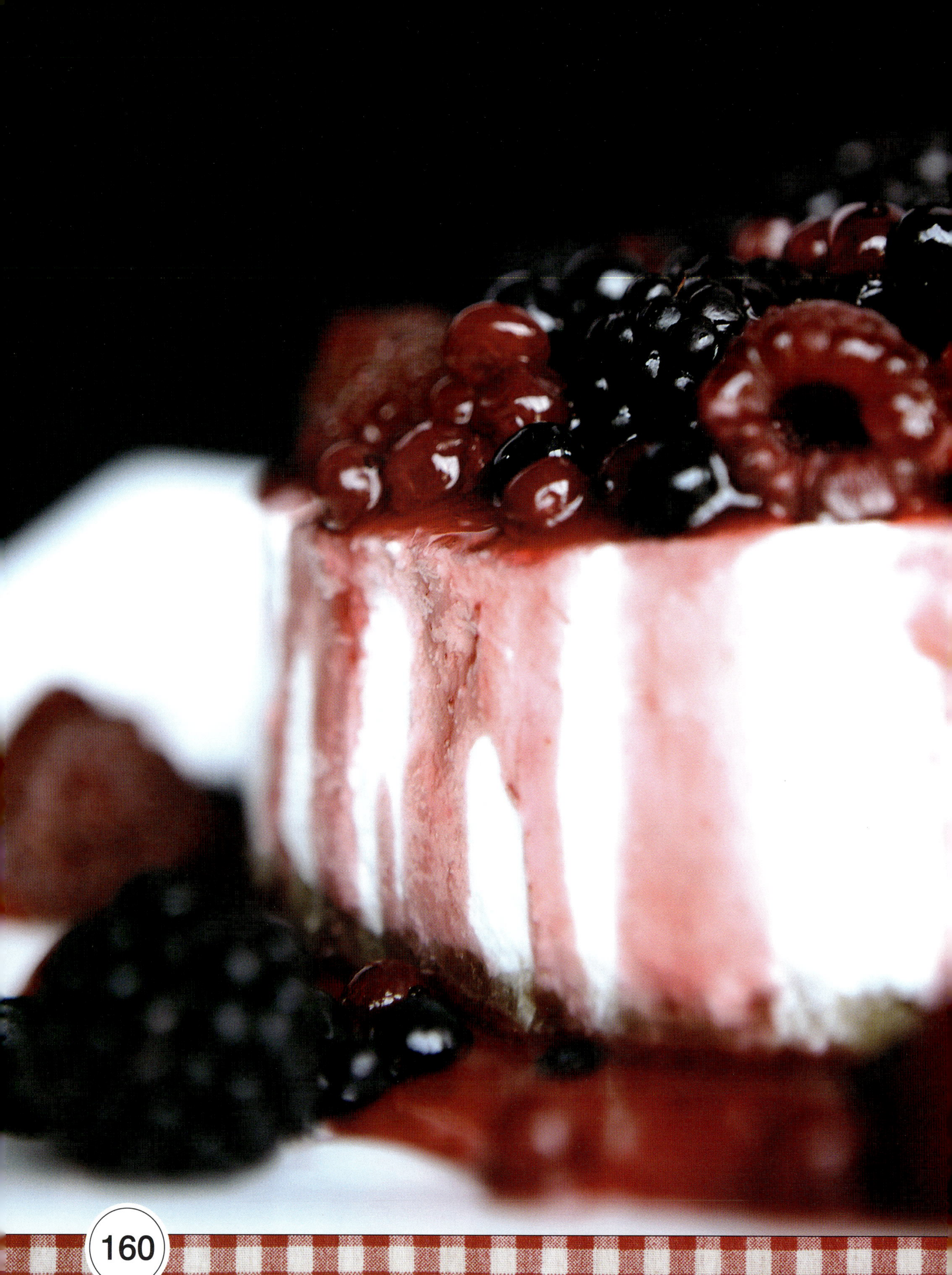

Creamy tofu cheesecake

½ cup couscous soaked in 1 cup boiling water
½ cup cashews
2 cups orange juice
½ cup honey or apple juice concentrate
2 Tbs cornflour
3 Tbs lemon juice
1 tsp vanilla
250g packet tofu

Blend the cashews smooth in just enough of the orange juice to cover them. Then add the other ingredients and blend briefly. Transfer the mixture to a saucepan and cook, stirring continuously, until it thickens. Pour onto a granola base and allow to cool. Serve as it is, or with fruit or agar jelly topping (see below or page 157). This cheesecake can also be baked: pour the uncooked mixture onto the base, smooth the top and cook in a moderately hot oven until it is solid (but not firm). Allow to cool before adding topping.

Fruit topping for cheesecakes – cook together 1 cup apple juice concentrate and 1 Tbs cornflour until it thickens. As it cools stir in 2-3 cups blackberries, raspberries or sliced strawberries. If more sweetening is needed, add a little honey or muscovado sugar. Spoon the topping onto the cheesecake just before serving.

Lemon cheesecake

If the filling is not sweet enough for your taste, reduce the lemon juice or increase the sweetening. It's quite small, so use a 7-inch (18cm) tin.

½ cup apple juice concentrate or honey
1½ Tbs cornflour
¼ cup oil
1 medium-sized lemon – rind and juice
¼ cup non-dairy milk
250g packet tofu

Blend first 5 ingredients together until very smooth, then add the tofu and blend again. The mixture should be a thick cream. Pour it onto a granola base, and bake in the oven until it is firm – about 20 minutes in a moderate oven.

Agar jelly topping – arrange thin lemon slices on cheesecake before pouring the topping over.
50ml water
½ Tbs agar flakes
4 Tbs apple juice concentrate or honey, or to taste
2 tsp lemon juice
Bring ingredients to the boil in a small saucepan, then gently pour over cheesecake. Allow to cool before serving.

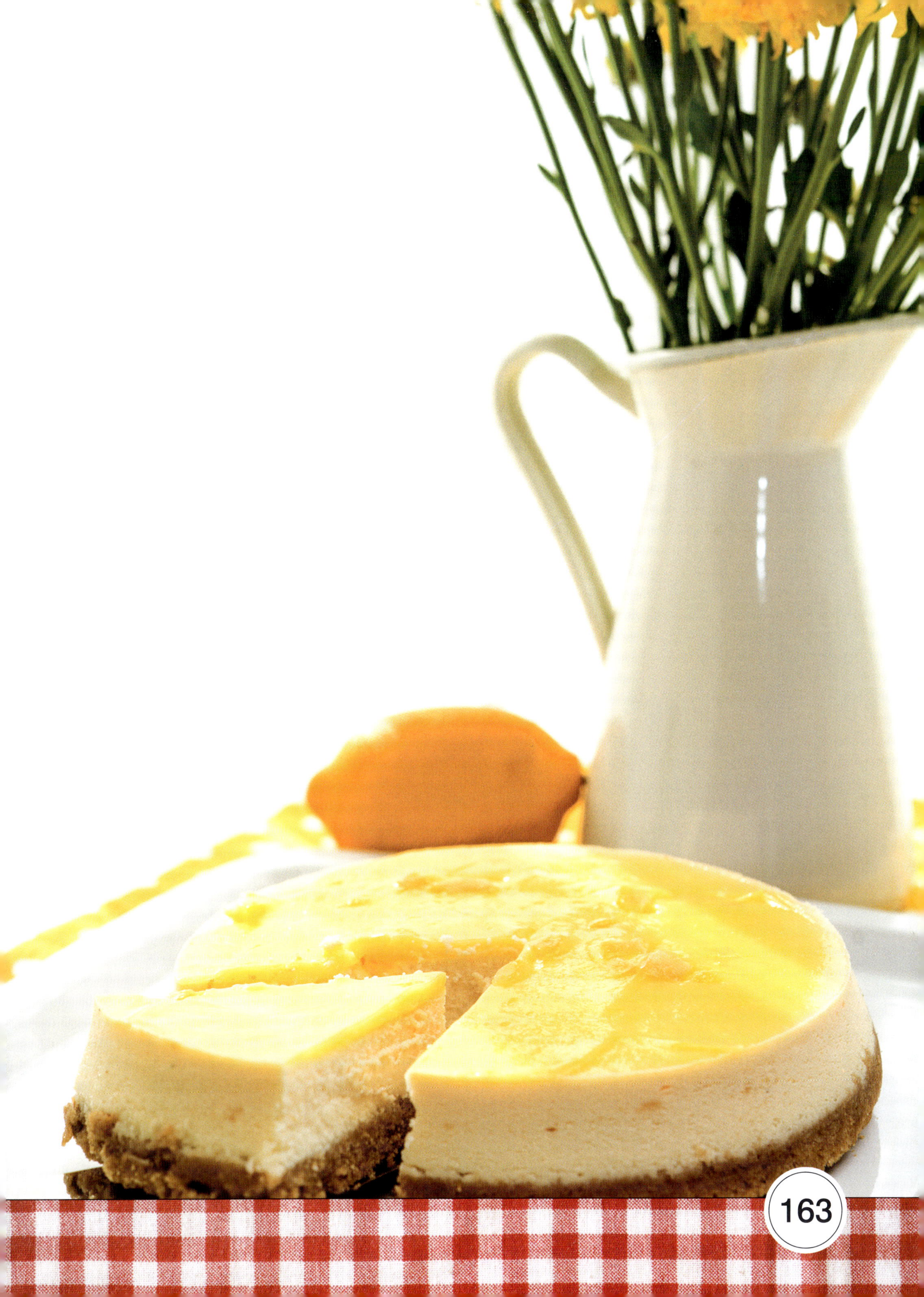

164

Danish apple cake

This is not a cake but a delicious pudding, made with layers of apple purée and crumb mixture, and topped with 'cream'.

Apple purée: this needs to be thick, so cook roughly chopped unpeeled apples in minimum water (blend if necessary), and sieve. There is no need to sweeten it if you use sweet apples such as Cox's. With sour cooking apples, sweeten to taste.

Crumb mixture A: 3 cups brown breadcrumbs, 1 cup desiccated coconut or ground nuts, ½ cup apple juice concentrate or liquid honey.
Crumb mixture B: the same except for 1 cup chopped dates instead of apple juice concentrate or honey. Put the chopped dates in the blender with the chunks of bread when you make the breadcrumbs.

Mix together well, spread on a baking tray and toast in a moderate oven until lightly browned.

Arrange layers of apple purée and crumb mixture in a deep glass bowl, starting and finishing with a crumb layer. Top with non-dairy 'cream'.

Tofu cream topping
½ cup cashews
1 Tbs honey or apple juice concentrate
½ 250g packet tofu
A few drops vanilla essence
½ cup non-dairy milk
1 Tbs lemon juice

Cook the cashews briefly in just enough of the non-dairy milk to cover them. Transfer to the blender and blend until smooth. Add everything except the lemon juice and blend briefly. Transfer to a bowl and very gently fold in the lemon juice, which will help to thicken the cream, and it will thicken further as it stands.

Fruit crumble

Traditional fruit crumbles use quite a lot of sugar, but you can use dates, raisins, or apple juice concentrate to sweeten. Here are some suggestions:
Apple and raisin
Rhubarb and date
Plum and blackberry with raisins

NB: Some fruits, particularly some apples, take longer to cook than the topping does, so partly cook them before you add the crumble topping.

When using dried fruit to sweeten, use one cup dried fruit to 2-3 cups fresh fruit, depending on how sweet the fresh fruit is. Add one cup water for each cup dried fruit plus 1-2 cups extra – depending on the size of the crumble. Fill your baking dish ½-⅔ full of fruit, spread the crumble over the top, and cook in a moderately hot oven until the crumble browns and the fruit is cooked.

Crumble topping A
1 cup wholewheat flour
1 cup rolled oats
¼ cup oil
Enough apple juice concentrate or honey to give it a crumbly consistency when mixed together lightly.

Crumble topping B
1 cup porridge oats
1 cup wholewheat flour
1 cup dates soaked in enough water to cover
1½ cups sunflower seeds, ground in blender

Mix it together, adding extra water if necessary to make it crumbly.

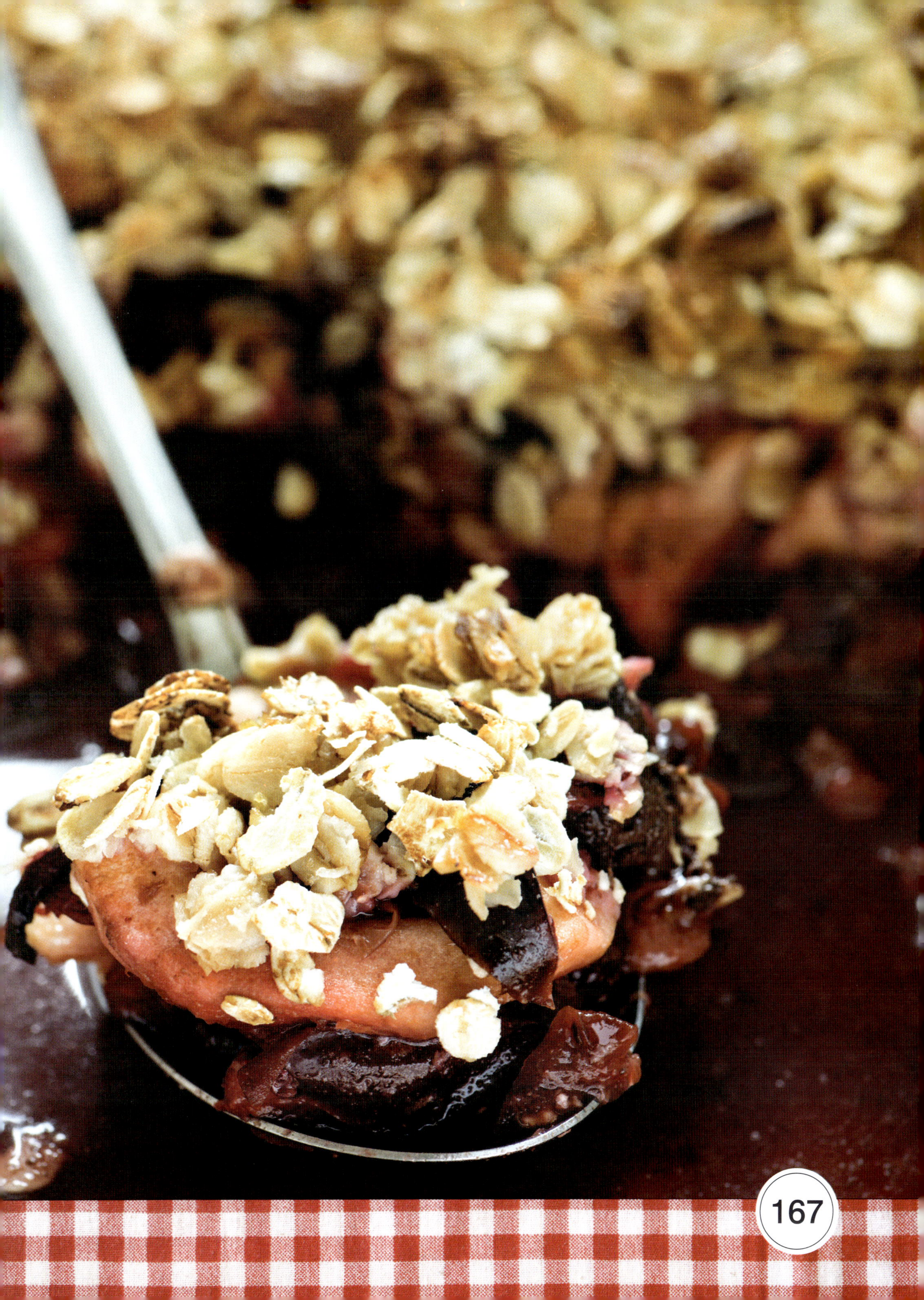

WAFFLES

Very good waffles can be made without milk or eggs. The ingredients can be varied, the one important principle being that the batter should be liquid enough to pour easily into the waffle iron, and thick enough to cook through before the outside gets too brown. Waffle batter thickens on standing, so, if you have time, let the batter stand for an hour or more. Otherwise, just add water as needed as it thickens up.

   Adding some oil or replacing some of the flour with ground sunflower seeds will make a crisper waffle. Waffles tend to go soggy as they stand, so if you are making them for a lot of people, make them a little in advance, and keep them crisp in the oven, or reheat them in the waffle iron just before serving. Waffles are good reheated for breakfast the next day.

Corn-oat waffles
3½ cups porridge oats
½ cup cornmeal
3½ cups water or milk
2 Tbs oil

Optional additions for sweet waffles:
¼ cup dates or 2 Tbs honey
Vanilla or maple flavouring

Additions for savoury waffles:
A small onion, roughly chopped
Your choice of herbs
Salt or herb salt to taste

Blend everything together for about 30 seconds. Pour into oiled and heated waffle iron and cook.

Tahini-oat waffles
2 cups water or milk
Vanilla or maple flavouring
2 cups porridge oats
1-2 Tbs honey or apple juice concentrate or 2-3 dates
2 Tbs tahini
Pinch of salt
2 Tbs wholewheat, barley or other flour

Let the batter stand and thicken, then add extra liquid as needed.
   Bake as for corn-oat waffles. Both recipes freeze well. The easiest way to thaw them is in a toaster.

Carob peanut butter topping for waffles
Cook together for 5 minutes:
½ cup water + ¼-½ cup carob powder
Transfer to blender and blend until smooth with ¼-½ cup dates softened in an equal amount of water, ½ cup peanut butter and a few drops vanilla flavouring.

What to eat with waffles

You can use them like bread, and spread them with anything savoury or sweet that you would spread on bread. For a dessert, serve them with any combination of maple syrup, apple sauce, whole-fruit jam, fruit spread, carob pie filling, sliced bananas and peanut butter topping (although not necessarily all at once!).

FRUIT SALADS

Here are a few suggestions for some different kinds of fruit salad. Different colours, flavours and textures make interesting fruit salads. Dried and fresh fruits can be used together, and nuts often make a good addition.

Date and apple:
Dice one dessert apple for each person. Add several chopped dates and walnuts for each apple. Serve at once, or pour a little orange or lemon juice over to keep apples from going brown.

Quick winter fruit salad:
Slice crisp, unpeeled eating apples, and add chopped, peeled oranges, a tin of pineapple chunks and, for texture and flavour, a handful of raisins.

Quick summer fruit salad:
Slice strawberries, bananas, nectarines, peaches or apricots, and sprinkle with toasted flaked almonds.

Eat fruit salads with soya cream, coconut milk, cashew cream, tofu cream topping (page 165), fruit cream or a smoothie.

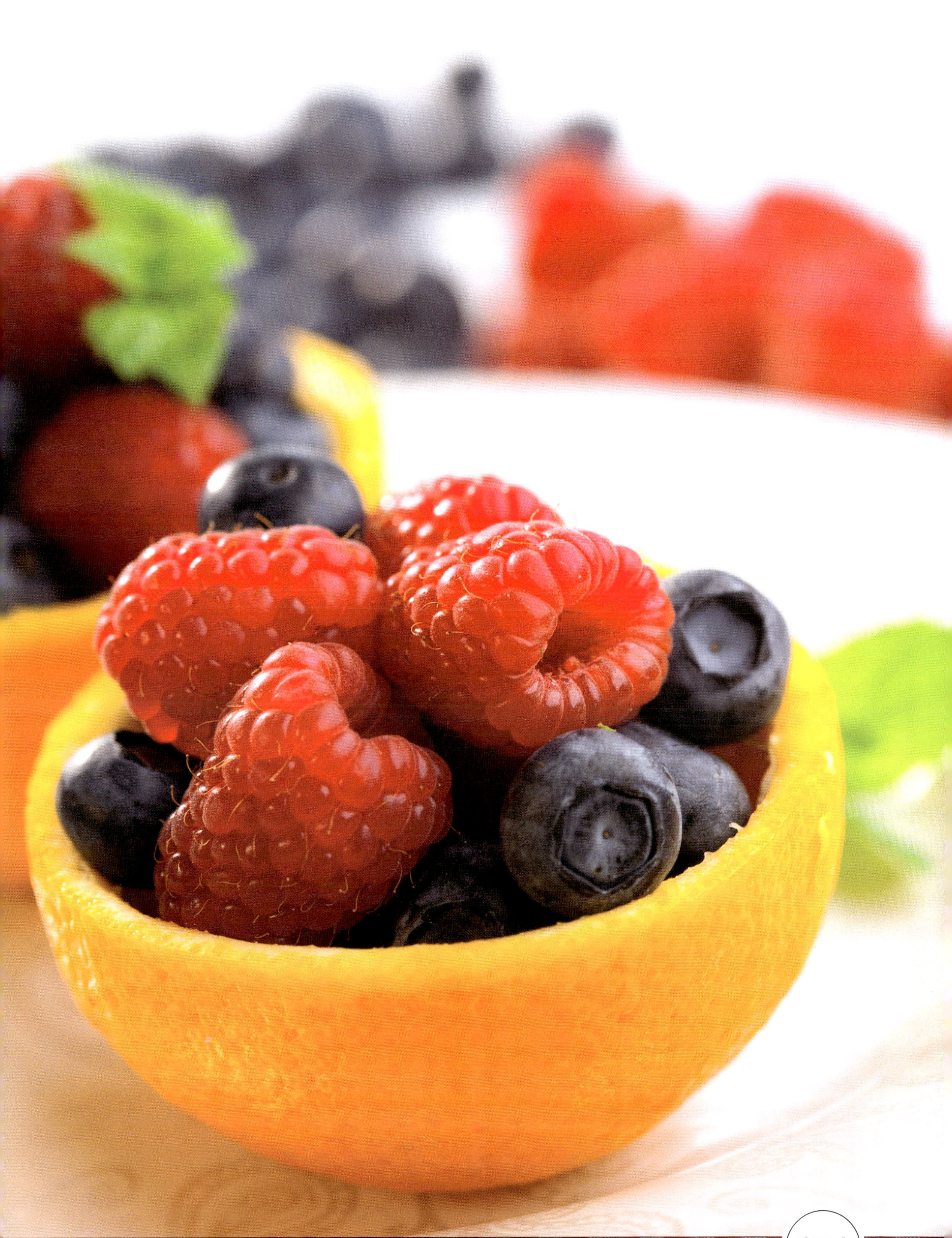

172

SMOOTHIES, LOLLIES, AND NON-DAIRY 'ICE CREAM'

Smoothies are very quick and easy to make, and very versatile. They can be liquid enough to drink through a straw or solid enough to eat with a spoon like soft ice cream. They can also be frozen as ice lollies, or an ice cream machine can transform them into sorbets or ice creams.

Fruit smoothie
Use any fruit and any juice. There should be enough juice to enable the blender blades to turn easily. You can use fresh fruit (reasonably small pieces), softened dried fruits or cooked or frozen fruits. Frozen bananas are very good. If berries with small, hard seeds are used, the smoothie should be sieved. If it needs to be sweetened, use dates, raisins, honey, or apple juice concentrate. Just blend it all together until smooth.

Some smoothie suggestions: frozen banana, orange juice, dried apricots; peaches and raspberries with apple juice; mango with orange juice.

'Cream' smoothie
Frozen bananas* cut in small chunks
'Cream' – this can be coconut milk, tofu, soya milk, cashews (be sure to blend them until smooth before adding other ingredients).
Fruit – any sort; berries or blackcurrants (strain out the seeds) are especially good in cream smoothies.

*To freeze bananas, remove skins, put in airtight bags or containers and freeze.

Fruit whips
Add a packet of tofu to a fruit smoothie mix and you have a quick and easy pudding to eat with crunchy cookies, or with a fruit salad. The recipe is very flexible; the exact proportions don't matter as long as it tastes good. You can serve it in individual dishes topped with toasted almond flakes, chopped nuts, pieces of fruit, or even granola.

Easiest possible apricot tofu whip
1 cup dried apricots cooked in orange juice
1 250g packet tofu
1-3 Tbs honey or apple juice concentrate if desired

Blend until smooth.

COOKIES, BISCUITS AND BARS

These recipes are all very wholesome, containing nothing refined, so they are very nutritious and a good choice for children's lunch boxes. They are very easy to make. Proportions need not be exact, and the choice of ingredients is flexible, too.

Date and coconut cookies
1 cup chopped dried dates, soaked in just enough water to cover them
1 cup sunflower seeds, ground in blender
1 cup desiccated coconut
1 cup rolled oats
½ tsp vanilla essence

Mix all ingredients together well and form into small balls, adding a little water if necessary. Place the cookies on an oiled baking tray and press them flat with a fork. Bake in a moderate oven until they are golden brown, then cool them on a wire rack. Makes 15-20 cookies.

Variations:
- You can use any seed, nut, dried fruit or flour, and any fruit juice instead of water.
- If you like it extra sweet, add an extra ½ cup dates, or add 1-2 Tbs apple juice concentrate, runny honey or malt extract. If this makes it too sticky, add a few more oats.

- You can use nuts instead of, or as well as, the coconut or sunflower seeds. Grind nuts in the blender first, or chop them finely.
- Try chopped dried apricots and/or raisins instead of dates, plus liquid to bind it. Apple sauce and mashed banana are two possibilities.
- If you like it spicy, add a teaspoonful of coriander seeds and a cardamom pod to the sunflower seeds in the blender.
- No blender? The cookies will just be more crumbly and chewy, but some prefer them like that anyway.

Bars: spread the mixture about 2cm thick on an oiled tray, and cut into bars or squares when cooked.

Thin, crisp biscuits
The ingredients are the same as for the cookies.

If you are using chopped dried dates, rather than softening them in water, grind them finely in the blender. This works best if you grind them with seeds or nuts. Add enough liquid to make a dough that you can roll out thinly, cut into circles or squares and bake in a moderate oven until crisp (10-15 minutes). Cool on a wire rack.

Apricot bars (papaya can also be used)
Crumb crust
4 cups rolled oats
½ cup honey
1 cup wholewheat flour
½ cup oil
1 cup desiccated coconut

Mix thoroughly. Place one half of the mixture in an oiled 8x12-inch (20x30cm) baking tin. Spread with filling. Cover with the rest of the crumb mixture, pressing it down lightly. Bake until light brown. Cut into bars when cool.

Apricot date filling:
Cook 3 cups dried apricots and 1 cup dates in enough water to cover them. When soft, blend coarsely.

Apricot orange filling:
Soak and cook 1 cup apricots in orange juice, then blend coarsely. Handheld blenders are best for small amounts of thick material.

Peanut butter or tahini flapjack
1 cup peanut butter or tahini
½ cup liquid honey
4 cups rolled oats

- Mix together thoroughly, press onto a flat baking tray (8 inches or 20cm square).
- Bake in a moderate oven until firm and golden brown. Cut into squares or bars while still hot.
- Cool on tray or wire rack.

Granola fruit bars
1 cup porridge oats
1 cup wholewheat flour
1 cup sunflower seeds

1 cup desiccated coconut
1 cup fruit – raisins, chopped dried apricots or dried cranberries
1 cup olive oil
¼ cup water
¼ cup soft brown sugar, malt, honey or apple juice concentrate. If you use sugar add an extra ¼ cup water.

Mix everything together thoroughly. If necessary, add a little extra water to make it stick together. Spread about ½ inch (1½ cm) deep in an oiled tray. Press down well and smooth the surface. Bake in a moderate oven until golden brown. Cut into bars while still hot, and allow to cool in tray.

SWEETS FOR FESTIVE MEALS

Mincemeat
The original mincemeat was made with meat, fruit and spices. The meat was omitted long ago, though some brands are still made with suet. Most commercial mincemeat is vegetarian now, but even the health food store varieties tend to be very sweet. Below is an all-fruit recipe from an old Scottish cookbook, which is quick and easy to make.

1 cup raisins
1 cup currants
½ cup mixed peel
1 cup chopped grapes
1 cup chopped apple
½ to 1 tsp mixed spice*
Grated lemon rind and juice

Add 1 cup water and cook together until apples and grapes are soft. It can be used as it is, or it can be minced or briefly blended first. If you prefer it sweeter, add apple juice concentrate to taste.

*Try coriander, cardamom and star anise for a different and delicious taste. Grind together 1 Tbs star anise, 1 Tbs coriander seed and ½ Tbs cardamom pods. Keep it in a jar and use as you would mixed spice.

Christmas mince tart
1 wholemeal pastry pie shell (10 inches/25cm)
1½ cups mincemeat
1 orange, cut in thin slices
Honey or apple juice concentrate

Spread a thick layer of mincemeat on the pie shell. Cover the mincemeat layer with thin slices of fresh oranges, and drizzle honey or apple juice concentrate over them. Bake until the pastry is cooked, or, if you use a pre-cooked pie shell, just bake until everything is thoroughly heated through. Serve warm with soya or other non-dairy cream.

Moroccan date and almond truffles
1½ cups toasted almonds
1 cup chopped dates
1 Tbs honey
½ tsp cinnamon

1 Tbs orange flower water

½ cup shredded coconut

- Grind the dates and almonds together in the blender.
- Remove from the blender and mix in the next three ingredients. You may need to add extra liquid if the dates are very dry. Form into small balls and roll in the shredded coconut.

Fruit squares
1 cup raisins
1 cup dried apricots
1 cup dates
½ cup nuts

2 Tbs lemon juice
2 Tbs honey
Rice paper

Mince the fruit and nuts in a food processor or mincer. Add the lemon juice and honey and mix well. It should be a very stiff paste. Spread it thickly (¾ inch-2cm) on rice paper. Smooth it with a rolling pin and cover it with another piece of rice paper. Place weight on top for several hours or overnight, and then cut into squares or bars.

Index

Agar 15, 46, 157, 161, 162
Apple pie 149
A quick clear soup 52
Baked oatmeal 29
Balkan bean soup 75
Basic savoury nut recipe 110
Bean and vegetable stew 103
Bean burgers 103
Beans 8, 75, 91, 98, 100, 103, 119, 134, 141, 142
   haricot 76, 79, 100, 103
   kidney 75, 99, 100
   mung 99
   soya 99, 104
Bean salad 91
Beetroot salad, cooked 88
   raw 86
Bobotie 127
Breads 39
Breakfast bread or rice pudding 22
Breakfasts 16
Bubble and squeak 45
Butter bean casserole 103
Butters 7, 19, 40
   avocado 40
   banana 41
   avocado banana 41
   nut 40
   seed 32, 40
Carob 158, 168
Carob peanut butter topping 168
Carob pie 158
Carrot and celeriac salad 86
Carrot and spinach pie 132
Carrot and sweet potato soup 56
Carrot salad 84
'Cheese' 15, 40, 45, 46, 47, 95, 108, 123, 135
Chestnut soup 59
Chickpeas 8, 48, 95, 98, 99, 100, 131
Coconut saffron rice 138
Cookies, biscuits and bars 174
   apricot bars 175
   date and coconut cookies 174
   thin, crisp biscuits 175
Corn salad 91
Country Life cashew pimento cheese 46
Creamed corn soup 64
Cream of broccoli stalk soup 67
Creamy tofu cheesecake 161
Crudités and dips 95
   garlic 'cream' dressing 93
   guacamole 95

hummus 95
   tofu cottage cheese 95
   tofu dips 95
Crunchy granola base 146
Curry channa/chickpeas 131
Cucumber salad 84
Dairy-free 30, 64
Danish apple cake 165
Desserts 144
Easy beans 44
Fats 14, 15, 40
Festive nut roast 116
Fillings, apricot date 176
   apricot orange 176
French apple tart 150
Fruit crisp topping 26
Fruit crumble 166
Fruit salads 170
   date and apple 170
   quick summer 170
   quick winter 170
Fruit spreads 42, 43
Fruit tart 157
Granola 32
Granola fruit bars 176
Green, white and orange salad 86
Guacamole 95, 134
Haystacks 134
Healthy spinach soup 63
Home-made baked beans 103
Hummus 48
Jams 10, 42, 43
Joffof rice 137
Lemon cheesecake 162
Lemon tart 153
Lentils 8, 55, 97, 115, 120, 127
Lentil soup 55
Lighter cheese sauce 123
Main meals 96
Mayonnaise 92
'Milk' 9, 15, 19, 36
Millet 21, 25, 32, 111
Millet crumble 25
Minestrone 76
Mixed vegetable cream soup 68
Moy moy 141
Muesli 30
Nut-free alternatives 120
   lentil roast 120
   sunflower and sesame roast 120
Nuts 8, 9, 14, 17, 18, 97, 110, 112, 115, 116

cashew 36, 46, 47, 56, 59, 63, 64, 67, 80, 87, 91, 93, 103, 115, 116, 123, 127, 134, 135, 170
hazelnuts 40, 111
peanuts 6, 11, 40, 111, 142
walnuts 22, 33, 40, 87, 111, 112, 116, 170
Nut roast en croûte 119
Nutty rice savoury 112
Nyoyo 142
Oats 8, 9, 20
Oils 40
olive 9, 15, 51, 146, 177
Omega-3 20
Organic 10
Pastry, 100% whole-food, no-oil 124
wholemeal (with oil) 124
wholemeal pastry crackers 124
Peanut butter or tahini flapjacks 176
Pineapple cream pie 154
Pitta pizza 47
Potage crème d'haricots 79
Potato salad 88
Pulses 8, 99
Pumpkin soup 72
Quick and easy spicy parsnip soup 60
Quick 'cheese' sauce 47
Quick vegan cheese sauce 123
Red lentil and cashew nut roast 115
Rice salad 91
Russian salad 88
Salad dressings 92, 95
Salads 82
citronette French dressing 92
garlic 'cream' dressing 93
oil-free citronette 93
soya manyonnaise 92
sunflower cashew cream 93
tofu mayonnaise 92
vegan sour cream 93
Sauces 45
Scrambled tofu 44
Seeds 9, 14, 17, 18, 32, 40, 87, 97, 99, 112
caraway 20, 21, 99
chia 20
flaxseed 19, 20, 21
pumpkin 8, 19, 32, 33, 40, 86, 87
sunflower 8, 32, 33, 35, 40, 46, 64, 67, 68, 71, 80, 86, 87, 93, 111, 120, 124, 134, 146, 166, 168, 174, 175, 176
Smoothies, lollies, and non-dairy 'ice cream' 173
'cream' smoothie 173
easiest possible apricot tofu whip 173

fruit smoothie 173
fruit whips 173
Soups 50
Soya 9, 13, 15, 19, 21, 36, 104, 108
Spinach cakes 128
Spreads, bean 48
English special 48
hummus 48
Mediterranean 48
tapenade 48
Sprinkle toppings 87
Sprouted seeds, alfalfa 87
mung 87
Sweeteners 14
Sweet pepper salad 84
Sweets for festive meals 178
Christmas mince tart 178
fruit squares 179
mincemeat 178
Moroccan date and almond truffles 178
Tabouli 90
Tahini 8, 10, 19, 35, 168
Tapenade 19, 48
To eat with soup 80
100% whole-food crackers 80
crispy crackers 80
croutons 80
garlic sour cream 80
sunflower or cashew cream 80
sunflower or cashew sour cream 80
Tofu 35, 36, 44, 92, 95, 104, 107, 108, 127, 161, 162, 165, 173
Tofu cottage cheese 104
Tofu lasagne 108
Tofu quiche 107
Tomatoes Provençal 45
Tomato cream soup 71
Tomato salad 84
Toppings 19, 45, 47, 87
Tossed salad 85
TVP 15, 108
Vegan 5, 45, 93, 97, 108, 123, 135
Vegan cheese 45, 123
Very easy beans 100
Waffles 35
corn-oat waffles 168
tahini-oat waffles 168
Winter salad 86

181

Juicing for Life

Beverley Ramages has become a regular fresh juice and smoothie maker, and this publication showcases over a hundred of her favourite recipes.

Along with these healthy, easy-to-make and tasty recipes, there is useful information on:
- Selecting the right equipment to get started,
- The values and benefits of the ingredients, and
- The health benefits of each recipe.

All of which will be useful as you begin to develop drinks for your own requirements – for example:
- Weight loss or gain,
- Energy boosting,
- Detoxing, or
- Ensuring that your family get their five-a-day.

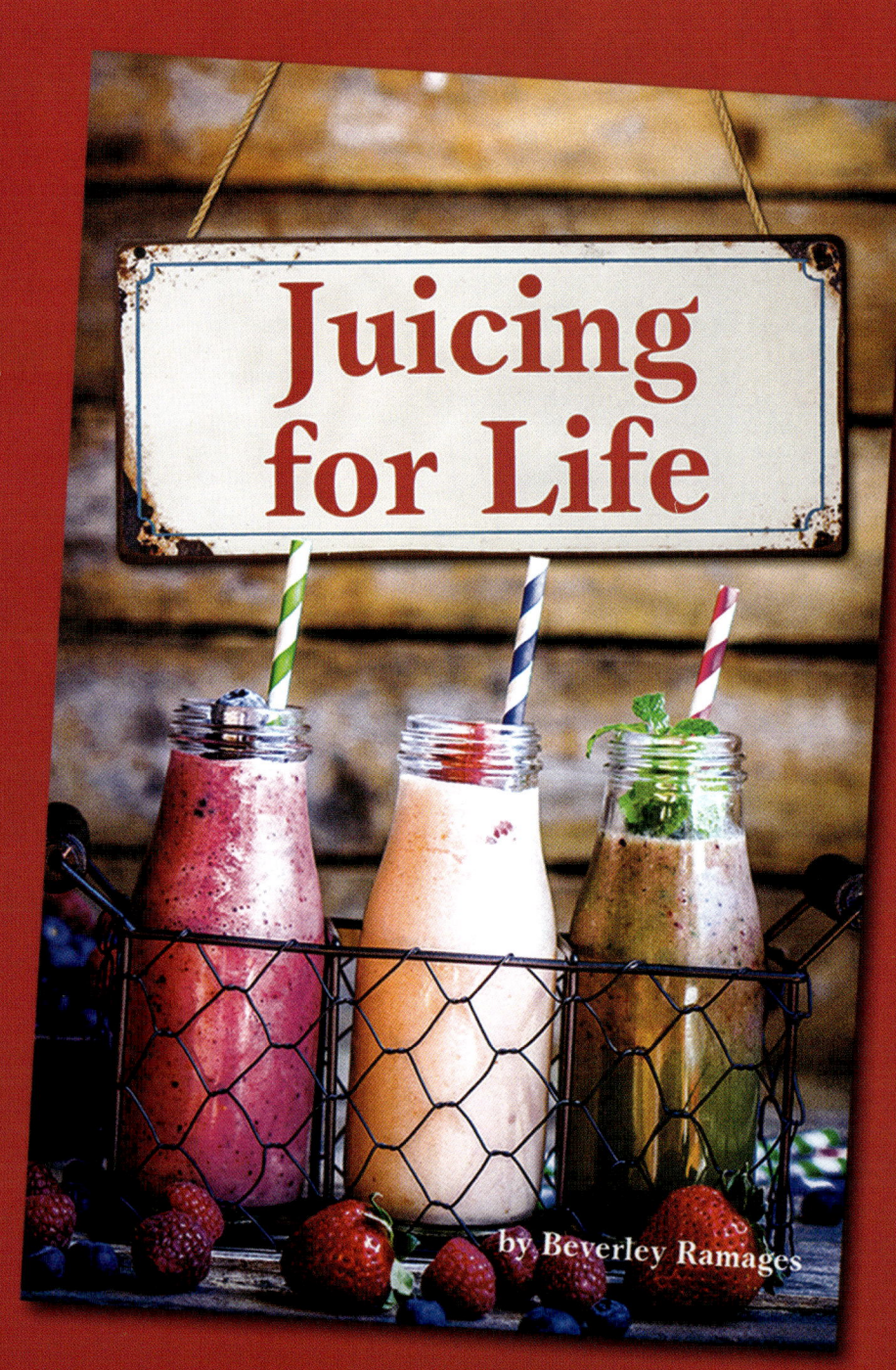

The Stanborough Press Ltd

Understanding Nutrition

Dr Clemency Mitchell has had 30 years in general medical practice, even longer teaching college students health principles, running health, nutrition and cookery courses.

'My years in general practice taught me that a change in diet and lifestyle would be by far the best prescription for most chronic health problems,' writes Dr Mitchell.

'Nowadays we are bombarded with information about health, including numerous nutritional theories that often seem to change from day to day.'

She continues, 'The principles underlying this book are not based on such shifting sand but on the age-old principles of the Bible, in particular the story of Creation in the book of Genesis where we learn that the Creator designed a plant-food diet and an active lifestyle with a weekly rest day for the human race.'

She concludes, 'Medical and nutritional science, common sense and experience both in the kitchen and the consulting room confirm that these principles still hold the secrets of good health.'

The Stanborough Press Ltd

Your Health In Your Hands

Lifestyle diseases are the biggest killers the Western world faces – and they're of increasing concern for the developing world, too. Your health, and the health of your family, is increasingly a matter of choice, not chance. Find out more about how to choose wisely in this fascinating book originated by a team of doctors and healthcare professionals.

The Stanborough Press Ltd